08.05.19

D1612406

THE
LITTLE
BOOK
OF
CORK
HARBOUR

KIERAN MCCARTHY

First published 2019

The History Press
The Mill, Brimscombe Port
Stroud, Gloucestershire, GL5 2QG
www.thehistorypress.co.uk

British Library Cataloguing in Publication Data.
A catalogue record for this book is available from the British Library.

ISBN 978 0 7509 8805 6

Typesetting and origination by The History Press
Printed by TJ International Ltd, Padstow, Cornwall

CONTENTS

ACKNOWLEDGEMENTS

My thanks to the editorial staff at The History Press Ireland and the staff of Cork City and County Libraries for their help. I would also like to thank Mairéad, my family and friends for their continued support.

ABOUT THE AUTHOR

For over twenty years, Kieran has actively promoted Cork's heritage with its various communities and people. He has led and continues to lead successful heritage initiatives through his community talks, City and County school heritage programmes, walking tours, newspaper articles, books and his work through his heritage consultancy business.

For the past nineteen years, Kieran has written a local heritage column in the *Cork Independent* on the history, geography and its intersection of modern day life in communities in Cork City and County. He holds a PhD in Cultural Geography from University College Cork and has interests in ideas of landscape, collective memory, narrative and identity structures.

Kieran is the author of twenty local history books: *Pathways Through Time, Historical Walking Trails of Cork City* (2001), *Cork: A Pictorial Journey* (co-written 2001), *Discover Cork* (2003), *A Dream Unfolding, Portrait of St Patrick's Hospital* (2004), *Voices of Cork: The Knitting Map Speaks* (2005), *In the Steps of St Finbarre, Voices and Memories of the Lee Valley* (2006), *Generations: Memories of the Lee Hydroelectric Scheme* (co-written, 2008), *Inheritance, Heritage and Memory in the Lee Valley, Co. Cork* (2010), *Royal Cork Institution, Pioneer of Education* (2010), and *Munster Agricultural Society, The Story of the Cork Showgrounds* (2010), *Cork City Through Time* (co-written, 2012), *Journeys of Faith, Our Lady of Lourdes Church Ballinlough, Celebrating 75 Years* (2013), *West Cork Through Time* (co-written, 2013), *Cork Harbour Through Time* (co-written, 2014), *Little Book of Cork* (2015), *North Cork Through Time* (co-written, 2015), *Ring of Kerry, The Postcard Collection* (2015), *Cork 1916: A Year Examined* (co-written, 2016), *Cork City Centre Tour* (2016) and *Secret Cork* (2017).

In June 2009 and May 2014, Kieran was elected as a local government councillor (Independent) to Cork City Council. He is also a member of the EU's Committee of the Regions.

More on Kieran's work can be seen at www.corkheritage.ie and www.kieranmccarthy.ie.

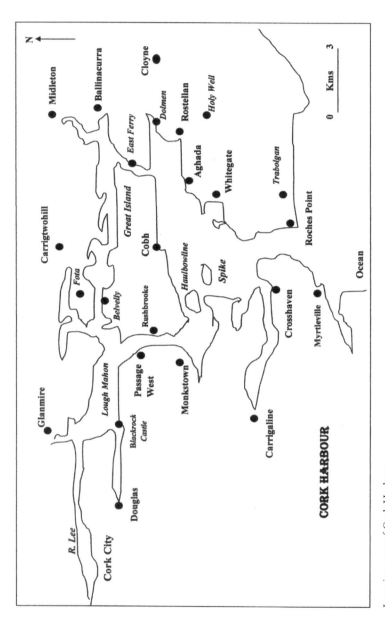

Location map of Cork Harbour

1

INTRODUCTION

THE TIDES OF TIME

Cork Harbour is a beautiful region of southern Ireland. It possesses a rich complexity of natural and cultural heritage. This is a little book about the myriad of stories within the second largest natural harbour in the world. It follows on from a series of my publications on the River Lee Valley, Cork City and complements the *Little Book of Cork* (The History Press Ireland, 2015). It is not meant to be a full history of the harbour region but does attempt to bring some of the multitude of historical threads under one publication. However, each thread is connected to other narratives and each thread here is recorded to perhaps bring about future research on a site, person or the heritage of the wider harbour.

The book is based on many hours of fieldwork and also draws on the emerging digitised archive of newspapers from the Irish Newspaper Archive and from the digitalised Archaeological Survey of Ireland's National Monument's Service. Both digitised sources have, more than ever, made reams and reams of unrecorded local history data accessible to the general public.

For centuries, people have lived, worked, travelled and buried their dead around Cork's coastal landscapes. The sea has been used as a source of food, raw materials, a means of travel and communications and a place of very distinct localities and communities. Some are connected to each other through recreational amenities such as rowing or boating and some exist in their own footprint with a strong sense of pride. Some areas, such as Cobh and the military fortifications, have been written about frequently by scholars and local historians; whilst some prominent sites have no written history, or just a few sentences accorded to their development.

Chapter 2, *Archaeology, Antiquities and Ancient Towers*, explores the myriad of archaeological finds and structures, which have survived from the Stone Age to post-medieval times. Five thousand years ago, people made their homes on the edges of cliffs and beaches surrounding the harbour. In medieval times, they strategically built castles on the ridges overlooking the harbour.

Chapter 3, *Forts and Fortifications*, explores the development of an impressive set of late-eighteenth-century forts and nineteenth-century coastal defences. All were constructed to protect the interests of merchants and the British Navy in this large and sheltered harbour.

Chapter 4, *Journeys through Coastal Villages*, takes the reader on an excursion across the harbour through some of the region's colourful towns. All occupy important positions and embody histories including native industries, old dockyards, boat construction, market spaces, whiskey making and food granary hubs. Each adds its own unique identity in making the DNA of the harbour region.

Houses, Gentry and Estates (Chapter 5) and *People, Place and Curiositie*s (Chapter 6) are at the heart of the book and highlight some of the myriad of people and personalities who have added to the cultural landscape of the harbour.

Chapter 7, *Connecting a Harbour*, describes the ways the harbour was connected up through the ages, whether that be through roads, bridges, steamships, ferries, or winch-driven barges. *Tales of Shipping* (Chapter 8) attempts to showcase just a cross-section of centuries of shipping which frequented the harbour; some were mundane acts of mooring and loading up goods and emigrants but some were eventful, with stories ranging from convict ships and mutiny to shipwrecks and races against time and the tide.

Chapter 9, *The Industrial Harbour*, details from old brickworks and ship building to the Whitegate Oil refinery. Every corner of the harbour has been affected by nineteenth-century and twentieth-century industries.

Chapter 10, *Recreation and Tourism*, notes that despite the industrialisation, there are many corners of the harbour where the Gaelic Athletic Association (GAA) and rowing can be viewed, as well as older cultural nuggets such as old ballrooms and fair grounds. This for me is the appropriate section to end upon. Cork Harbour is a playground of ideas about how we approach our cultural heritage, how we remember and forget it, but most of all how much heritage there is to recover and celebrate.

Enjoy!

Kieran McCarthy

2

ARCHAEOLOGY, ANTIQUITIES AND ANCIENT TOWERS

The Mesolithic Harbour

About ten thousand years ago, the first human settlers – hunter-gatherers of the Mesolithic or Late Stone Age era – came to Cork Harbour. Just over twenty-five shell midden sites are marked on maps created by the Archaeological Inventory of Cork Harbour – some of these have not survived; some survive just in local folklore. Some have been excavated throughout the twentieth century. There have also been unrecorded sites eroded away by the tide or by cliff collapse. Shell midden sites consist of refuse mounds or spreads of discarded seashells, and are normally found along the shoreline. Shellfish were exploited as a food source and sometimes as bait or to make dye. In Ireland, shell middens survive from as early as the Late Mesolithic period, but many of the Cork Harbour oyster middens have also been dated to medieval times, while some have produced post-medieval pottery dates.

Some of the shell middens are very extensive; for example, on a beach at Curlane Bank in Ringaskiddy, a lens of midden material extends for 30m north–south along the shoreline just above high tide mark, and measures 0.1m in thickness. The deposit contains cockles, limpets and winkles with some oyster and razor shells. At Ballintubbrid West, to the south west of Midleton, it is about 50m in length and over 1.5m thick.

Over a quarter of all identified middens in the Cork Harbour area are to be found at eight locations in Carrigtwohill parish. Brick lsland, in the estuary to the north of Great Island, is joined to mainland by narrow neck of land. When surveyed by the archaeologist Reverend Professor Power in 1930, the midden measured 5 or 6ft thick at the terrace edge and extended along the foreshore for over 180 yards, and inland for 70 or 80ft. It contained almost purely oyster shells with occasional cockle, mussel, whelk and other marine shells. Thin layers of charcoal were visible in many places and stone pounders or shell openers.

In 2001, archaeological monitoring of a 15-hectare greenfield site at Carrigrenan, Little Island, was carried out prior to the construction of a waste water treatment plant by Cork Corporation. Two shell spreads along the western seashore perimeter of the site were noted. A polished stone axe was recovered during topsoil monitoring and has been given a possible late Mesolithic date. All other finds were random pottery, eighteenth to twentieth century in date.

Smaller middens, for example at Currabinny, Currabally and Rathcoursey, reflect shorter periods of use. At the western end of Carrigtwohill in 1955, archaeologist M.J. O'Kelly (prior to the construction of a new school) excavated oyster shells, a few animal bones and fragments of glazed pottery dating to the late thirteenth/ early fourteenth century.

The Bell-Beaker Pottery Sherd

During the preparation works for Mahon Point Shopping Centre in 2003, an area of prehistoric activity was identified during testing by archaeologists Sheila Lane & Associates, in a development area known as Zone C. Features revealed during the excavation included a hearth surrounded by fifty stake-holes. Further west again, seven pits were found. A number of finds were recovered from them, including a possible quartz scraper, a fragment of a small flint bladelet, a flint flake, a type of flint plano-convex slug knife, two pieces of amethyst (one of which has a usable cutting edge), and a small shard of possible Bell Beaker pottery. The Bell Beaker culture, *c.* 2900–1800 BC, is the term for a widely scattered 'archaeological culture' of prehistoric western Europe, starting in the late Neolithic or Chalcolithic and running into the early Bronze Age.

Postholes of Prehistory

In 1992, a significant Bronze Age settlement was discovered at Fota Island. The archaeological investigation there began at the invitation of the developer, and lasted for a total of ten weeks. It was carried out under the aegis of Archaeological Development Services Ltd, Dublin, initially as a watching brief in advance of the construction of a golf course. Definite archaeological remains were found in nine separate areas during the construction work, at depths varying between 0.2m and 0.4m below the topsoil horizon. Three of these could be dated to the prehistoric period, and were fully excavated.

The first, Area 1, proved to be a porched house site of probably Bronze Age date. It consisted of a hearth, two large and amorphous pits, two stake slots, ten regularly cut post holes, and a number of shallow depressions and stake holes.

The second site, Area 4, occupied the summit of a low rise in the middle of the island. It consisted of fourteen pits of varying capacities. Its date is likely to be similar to, or slightly older than, the house in Area 1. The large oval pit in the middle of the site had survived to a depth of almost 1in and had been clay-lined twice during the course of its life. A post hole in the base of the pit may mean that a wooden gantry or platform was raised over it. Several humanly struck flints were recovered, a rare commodity on Fota, but the presence of two whetstones from a nearby feature may indicate that bronze blades were being sharpened in the vicinity. The four-posted structure may have been a grain platform.

Bronze Age Carrigaline

In 2014, Archaeologist Rob O'Hara discovered three Bronze Age-dated pits at Kilmoney, Carrigaline. Located in the floodplain of the Owenboy River, the published report denotes that in each pit charcoal and heat-fractured stone were present. A sample of alder charcoal was radiocarbon dated and showed activity on the site between 2456 BC and 2205 BC.

Carrignafoy's Cooking Complex

An excavation of a large fulacht fia, a Bronze Age cooking site, took place in April–May 2007 at Carrignafoy, on the north-east outskirts of Cobh. A spread of burnt stone, approximately 18m by 20m, was noted during site clearance at a greenfield development site, County Cork. As the development was already under way, full excavation of the site was recommended by the local authority. The site was located at *c*. 60m above mean sea level on the east slope of a 91m-high hill, which dominates the town of Cobh.

The uppermost level of the spread of burnt and heat-shattered stone was removed to reveal a trough connected by a shallow channel to two further troughs, all of which had been cut into the natural boulder clay. The sides of the trough were lined with a rough layer of sandstones, and two horizontal oak timbers were recorded at the base of the trough. A circular structure enclosed the trough. It was 5m in diameter and consisted of a series of seven post-holes, slot-trenches and stake-holes.

Eskers, Migrations and the Castle Mary Tomb

The eastern region of Cork Harbour became well known to archaeologists because of the number of chance finds discovered during the late nineteenth century and early twentieth century. The researches and publications of three scholars, T.J. Westropp, Rev P. Canon Power and M.J. O'Kelly, are still prominent sources for research. The former dealt with the headland forts along its coast and the latter with some of the place-names and antiquities in the inland terrain. Professor M.J. O'Kelly, in his 1945 publication in the *Journal of the Cork Historical and Archaeological Society*, states that the stone circles and alignments, which occur frequently in the west of County Cork, are entirely absent in the harbour region. However, there are but two chambered tombs in the area.

Professor O'Kelly explained that the dearth of chambered tombs in the section of Cork Harbour can be explained by environmental conditions in Bronze Age Ireland. At the time of greatest colonisation by the tomb-builders, the limestone river plains of the south occupying the east–west synclinal folds were very heavily forested, and this applied especially to the lower valleys of the Lee and Blackwater. The material equipment of the society of the Late Mesolithic Age could make but a little impression upon the dense woodlands of east Cork. So people migrated westward to the open uplands where, without any preliminary clearance of the ground, they were able immediately to practise early forms of agriculture and herding. Early Bronze Age settlers, though, somehow found a foothold near the coast at the western end of the Cloyne valley.

Professor O'Kelly outlines that an esker (an outcome of the melting Glaciation epoch) consisting of a series of detached mounds and ridges of gravel, runs from the eastside of the Castlemary demesne along the Saleen depression to Cork harbour. The esker would constitute an area of light soil unlikely to have supported a dense growth of timber in Bronze Age times; the two tombs are located upon or very near these gravels. Their position so near the coast suggests that this was the point of entry of at least one group of the early colonists.

The Castle Mary tomb must once have been an imposing monument. Its present state is not due to accidental collapse but to the deliberate clearing away of its earthen covering mound and the removal and breaking up of the stones of the tomb. There are now five stones on the site, four of which are side-stones of the chamber and the fifth a very large capstone. No trace of the small closed eastern chamber usually found in this type of tomb now exists. The wedge-shaped tomb belongs principally to the south and west of Ireland. The classic example of the tomb type for the whole country lies at Labbacallee, near Fermoy, County Cork.

Castlemary tomb, 1875 from M. Cusack, *A History of Cork* (source: Cork City Library)

The Mystery of the Rostellan Dolmen

To Cork and Irish archaeologists, the reasons behind the construction of the dolmen in Rostellan is a mystery. It has three upright stones and a capstone, which at one time fell down but was later re-positioned. It has a similar style to portal tombs but such style of tombs are not common at all to this region of the country. For the visitor, the site is difficult to access. The beach upon it sits gets flooded at high tides and access across the local mudflats is difficult and dangerous. It is easier to get to it with a guide through the adjacent Rostellan wood. The dolmen maybe a folly created by the O'Briens, former owners of the adjacent estate of Rostellan House on whose estate an extensive wooded area existed. The house was built by William O'Brien (1694–1777) the 4th Earl of Inchiquin in 1721. Notably, on the former estate grounds there is a definitive folly in the shape of a castle tower, named Siddons Tower, after the Welsh-born actress Sarah Siddons.

The Giant's Circle

The name Curraghbinny in Irish is *Corra Binne*, which is reputedly named after the legendary giant called Binne. Legends tells that his cairn (called a *corra* in Irish) is located in a burial chamber atop the now wooded hill. The cairn is not marked in the first edition Ordnance Survey map, but its existence was noted during the original survey in the Name Books compiled at that time. John Windle, the well-known Cork writer and antiquarian of the early nineteenth century, mentions the site in his publications. There is no record, though, in his printed works or in his manuscripts preserved in the Royal Irish Academy Library of any digging having taken place at the cairn.

In 1932, archaeologist Seán P.Ó. Riordáin and his team excavated the cairn. On beginning work, he found the cairn was thickly overgrown with bracken and brambles. He measured the diameter as about 70ft, and its greatest height was 7½ft above that of the surrounding area. The excavation was carried out by cutting off the cairn in narrow vertical sections parallel to an arbitrary base line to the east of the monument.

Except for a slight outer accumulation of soil, the cairn was composed of stone, most of which was local sandstone, there being only two pieces of limestone. As O'Riordáin's team worked into the cairn, several large boulders lying on the ground came into view. It soon became apparent that the boulders formed part of a circle running concentric with the outer edge of the mound.

As the archaeologists worked nearer the centre they found a further series of stones lying *in situ* on the clay floor of the cairn. These were found to form the arc of a circle, and the stones used were smaller than those of the outer circle, and less continuous, since part of the line was formed by an irregular mass of stones and clay.

On one flat stone forming part of the inner arc they found a group of about one hundred pebbles, water-rolled, and such as would come from a brook, while a second group of about sixty pebbles was found just north of the western end of the arc. At the centre of the mound they came upon a peculiar structure of stones and clay. The clay was raised to a height of about 4in above the surrounding surface, and the stones were embedded in it.

Beyond a thick deposit of charcoal, nothing was found among the stones, though two teeth and a piece of cow bone were found above them. The finds yielded by the cairn were few. A small bronze ring, about five-eighths of an inch in diameter, was found outside the kerb on the south-east side. Shells, mostly oyster with some cockle, were found at various depths varying from 9in under the surface of the cairn down to 6in above ground level.

The most interesting discovery was made on the south side of the cairn. In a space between two stones of the kerb and a third lying just inside it the team found, mixed with a thick layer of charcoal, some burnt bone fragments. Examination proved these to be human. The charcoal deposit with which the bones were found mixed did not extend under the neighbouring large stones. This showed that the fire was lit after the boulders had been placed in position. The cremated human bone found nearby was carbon dated roughly to be 4,000 years old.

The Legend of Neimheidh

The Annals of the Four Masters relate that one of the first colonists of Ireland was Neimheidh, who sailed into Cork Harbour over 1,000 years BC. One colourful tale holds that he was a descendant of Noah. The Great Island was known in Irish as Oileán Ard Neimheadh because of its association with him. Later it became known as Crích Liatháin because of the Lehane tribe who were rulers of it. It subsequently became known as Oileán Mór An Barra, (the Great Island of Barry & Barrymore) after the Barry family who inherited it. Local folklore records that a 15ft-high mound barrow grave existed on a hilltop at Corbally on Great Island, 1km north of Ballymore. It is said to mark the burial spot of Neimheadh. The barrow was sadly levelled in the 1890s, at which time three graves containing human remains were found.

The Cork Horns

The Cork Horns artefacts were discovered in reclamation deposits near the south jetties in the Victoria Road area of Cork city in 1909. When the excavations for a large tank had gone below river level, and while the workmen were working in water, one of them brought up on his shovel a very slender metal cone. Later in the day, two other similar cones, attached by metal to each other, were dug up at the same place. From a study of several of the old maps of Cork City, it is clear that in early times this particular area was a tidal salt marsh, if not an actual mud flat. Some mud inside the horns resembled the grey mud of slobland along the river. Two of the cones were joined by metal to each other. It appears that the horns were, in fact, helmet ornaments and perhaps date from the Iron Age. The horns are now on public display in Cork Public Museum.

The Kilmoney Ringfort

In 2002, Cork County Council commenced the construction of forty houses at Kilmoney, Carriagline. Monitoring of the initial breaking of the ground was needed. In the subsequent and published archaeological report by Catyrn Power, she did not find any objects or extra features. The ringfort was also cleared of overgrowth and the County Council took the decision to preserve and protect the fort for exploration and appreciation by the general public.

A Round Tower and its Cathedral

The foundation of the See of Cloyne was established by St Colman, who died in AD 604. In AD 707, an abbey was constructed on the west side of the cathedral, which was raided in 978 by the people of Ossory, and again, in 1089, by Dermot, the son of Fiordhealbhach O'Brien. The tower is unique as it is one of only two round towers in County Cork, which have survived the test of time (the other in Kinneigh near Enniskeane in West Cork). The sandstone tower has a suggested construction date of tenth–eleventh century AD and is over 30m high and 5.17m in diameter at the base. Its foundations are on a rocky outcrop, which is evident from the west side. Round towers are described by archaeologists as ecclesiastical bell towers and storage spaces. At one time there were over seventy round towers in the country. In the Cloyne tower, internal ladders provided access for a bell ringer to get to the bell floor of the towers.

On another site of older monastic buildings St Colman's Cathedral was built. The building dates from the thirteenth century. The Berkeley Chapel in the North Transept contains a marble effigy of the distinguished philosopher and Kilkenny-born George Berkeley, who was Bishop of Cloyne 1734– 1753. In 1709, he published *An Essay Towards a New Theory of Vision*. In this book, Berkeley set out his theory on Immaterialism, which is about the boundaries of human vision. His theory was that the proper objects of sight are not material objects but comprise light and colour.

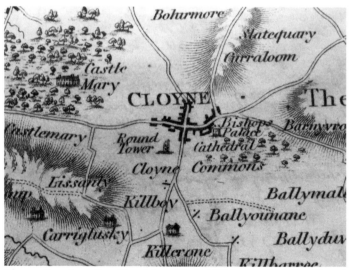

Cloyne village, from Grand Jury Map of Cork, 1811 (source: Cork City Library)

Postcard of Cloyne Round Tower,
*c.*1900 (source: Cork City Museum)

St Colman's Cathedral is a significant historical structure in the Cork Region. Through the centuries it has experienced several additions and reductions. Up to the year 1706 there were battlements on the walls of the nave which were then thought to be too weighty and thus taken down, moving the style of the building away from its original appearance. There is evidence that there was at one time a tower at the juncture of the transepts. Previously the Cathedral of the Diocese of Cloyne, it is now one of three cathedrals in the Church of Ireland United Dioceses of Cork, Cloyne and Ross.

Belvelly Castle

Built by the Hodnett family in the fifteenth century, Belvelly Castle is located on a very narrow piece of land on Great Island, bound by Belvelly bridge on one side and the shore on the other. This typical medieval four-storey square tower was the only castle of the Hodnett family in Cork.

The Hodnetts, a Shropshire family, appeared on the Great Island shortly after the Anglo–Norman Invasion. They built Belvelly castle to guard the entrance to the island. They acquired land near Carrigtwohill at Ballyannon and Ballyvodock and built two further castles. A branch of the Hodnett family founded Courtmacsherry.

On Great Island the Hodnetts remained undisputed lords of the adjacent territory until the end of the fourteenth century, when the Barrys and the Roches were gaining in power. On 16 May 1329, the castle was besieged by the combined forces of the Barrys and the Roches and, after a fierce conflict which lasted many days, the castle was taken, Lord Philip Hodnett and 140 of his men-at-arms being slain. After the siege the lands of Great Island fell into the hands of the Barrys, in whose possession it was for centuries.

In 1807–09, a bridge was built across the bay and thus Great Island lost its island status. Early in the nineteenth century Garret Barry owned Belvelly Castle. The Shaws bought it in 1859. Smith Barry bought it later and it remained in their ownership until 1984. A Frenchman named Gilles Darnieges bought it from Smith Barry and he established a Society of the Friends of Belvelly Castle Trust to restore it. Unfortunately, he was transferred to North Korea, as he was attached to the French Embassy, and his restoration plans were shelved. It was last occupied in the military sense during the Second World War. A number of window lights were replaced by horizontal concrete slits, built by the Irish Army during World War II. In 2018, the tower was undergoing restoration with an aim to return to being a private residence.

Barryscourt Castle, from Cork Camera Club archives, *c.*1900 (source: Cork City Museum)

Belvelly Castle, from Cork Camera Club archives, *c.*1900 (source: Cork City Museum)

Blackrock Castle

Blackrock castle was built in 1582 by the citizens of Cork to safeguard ships against pirates, who would come into the harbour and steal away the vessels. Its position overlooks a strategic point where the River Lee meets Lough Mahon as the river begins to widen towards the harbour estuary. Another reason for building a fort was the fear of a Spanish invasion. Spain for a long time posed a serious threat to the British Empire. The King, James I, could see clearly that Ireland could be used as a platform for attacks on Britain. In 1604, England's Lord Deputy Mountjoy defended himself against the citizens of Cork, who were rebelling against King James I of England. The Deputy wanted the citizens to acknowledge their new monarch. In 1608, the citizens of Cork regained the fort at Blackrock because of James I's first charter. Indeed Cork, Youghal and Kinsale, with several other towns in Munster, obtained new charters from the King which gave the local authority and people further privileges. The fort, which was then a circular tower, was used as a beacon light from a turf fire to guide shipping.

In 1722, the old tower was destroyed by fire and a new one built by the citizens. Again, the new tower was circular and was used as a beacon on top of an adjoining tower. Apart from functioning as a type of lighthouse, Admiralty Courts were held at Blackrock Castle. It was in 1759 that the first court of this kind was held there. It was also the court's job to organise an important ceremony called Throwing the Dart. This was an ancient rite by which the Mayor of Cork threw a metre-long dart into the water of Cork Harbour in order to show his authority over the port and harbour.

With the arrival of the second decade of the nineteenth century, Blackrock Castle was to be used once again as a festive meeting place by the corporation. But disaster struck when the second building was destroyed in 1827 by a fire. The rebuilding of this ancient castle commenced in 1828 and was completed on 3 March 1829. It incorporated into its basement the canon room of the seventeenth-century tower. The building that now stands consists of a large circular tower with a crenellated parapet. To the rear are several low buildings in the same style with entry gates, a courtyard and restaurant. A historical plaque details members of the Admiralty Court and sponsors who were involved in the construction of the third building. It can be found at the entrance of castle grounds. The current building has now been developed as an astronomy centre and museum exploring the history of the Universe and Irish scientists, and now boasts a state-of-the-art telescope observatory on the site. The site has a close working relationship with Cork Institute of Technology and Cork City Council.

Blackrock Castle, 1843 from *Illustrated London News* (source: Cork City Library)

The Rock of Carrigaline

The rock of Carrigaline Castle, upon which it stands, appears to have given its name to the adjacent village. Authorities differ as to its interpretation, some holding that it simply means 'the rock of O'Leidhin', or 'the rock of Lyne'; others say that it derives its name from the Hy-Liatháin, a sept who in pre-Anglo–Norman days held the district lying north and east of Cork Harbour.

In 1206, Anglo–Norman Philip de Prendergast was initially granted by King John the territory from the Walled Town of Cork to Innishannon. Further tracts of land were given soon after. Philip's grand-daughter married John de Cogan, Lord of Castlemore, and she brought to the Cogans the Prendergast lands in Carrigaline, at Castlelyons and Shandon. Carrigaline now became the principal home of the de Cogans. The castle remained in the hands of the family until Joan, daughter to the Lord Cogan of Carrigaline, married Maurice Fitz John Fitzgerald, and brought into the Desmond family the manors of Carrigaline, Carrigrohane and Castlemore. Her husband was slain at the Battle of Calian by the McCarthys in 1261.

By 1350, when the English at home were fully occupied with the War of the Roses, the Irish in Munster started to rally against the English overlords. The de Cogans in Carrigaline looked around for allies and in 1439 gave the overlordship of all their lands in County Cork to the Fitzgeralds, the Earls of Desmond, so that, instead of holding directly from the English king, they held them from the Earls of Desmond, who would be at hand to help them defend their property.

In 1562, Gerald, the heir to the earldom of Desmond, was in prison in London, short of money and weary of his imprisonment. To get money, he mortgaged the barony of Kerrycurrihy to Sir Warham St Leger, who had large plans for the plantation of Munster, with English settlers and the building of new towns which would be linked with the expanding English colonies in North America.

A difficulty arose with the district of Carrigaline. A lease had been given of Carrigaline and some other lands in Kerrycurrihy to Maurice Fitzgerald twenty years before by his brother, James, who was 13th Earl of Desmond. Maurice's two sons had grown up there, Thomas and the famous James Fitzmaurice Fitzgerald. Naturally they would resent anyone taking over the family castle. Therefore, when Sir Warham St Leger came to take possession of the castle in 1569, and other English settlers were moving into the lands of Tracton, James Fitzmaurice and MacCarthy Mór led 2,000 horsemen and laid siege to Tracton, which they captured. They then went on to re-take Carrigaline Castle.

On 9 November 1569, Sir Henry Sidney, deputy of Queen Elizabeth in Ireland, laid siege to Carrigaline Castle, which surrendered after resistance. Sidney put Barnaby Daly in charge of a garrison there as constable of the castle. Four years after the capture of Carrigaline Castle by Sidney, Barnaby Daly reported that, during those four years he had been many times assailed by Fitzmaurice and by John FitzRedmond Fitzgerald.

Although not fully proven, it is believed Carrigaline Castle was severely damaged during the Cromwellian Campaign in Ireland in the middle of the seventeenth century. It appears to have become ruinous from around 1700. The remains at present existing in the rock consist of two towers, which once guarded the eastern angles of a spacious courtyard.

The Cross of St John

The alleged site of the first Anglo–Norman settlement at Crosshaven in the thirteenth century was at Old Point. Guarded by a castle and linked with a larger manor, a small settlement grew. Crosshaven derived its name from a cross created in honour of St John near the settlement. Crosson is the earliest written form of the name (1301). In the year 1307 AD a law case highlights that Thomas le Husser of Crosshoun was summoned by Richard Heruy and Adam Grousmound, executors of Adam Henry's will, on a plea of a debt that was owed. Fast forward in time to the nineteenth century and Castle Point was an embarkation space called the Old Quay. In addition, the Castle Point village comprised just over twenty small cabin-type houses. Today, the Old Point settlement is built upon by modern housing and the Crosshaven boatyard, which provides much employment. On 15 December 2007, local historian and author Diarmuid Ó Mhurcadha did the honours of unveiling of a commemorative plaque near the alleged site of the castle.

Anastasia's Monkstown Castle

Located at the side of a steep glen overlooking the inner harbour, the entrance to Monkstown Castle was near the old Monkstown–Cork road. Circa 1636, according to legend, the lady who built Monkstown castle for 4d was Anastasia Archdeacon, wife of John Archdeacon, a member of an Anglo–Irish family. Anastasia's maiden name was Gould. She was a member of an old walled town of Cork family who were merchant princes. While he was serving abroad she was tasked with her husband's sum of money to oversee the construction of a new castle for the couple. Local folklore relates that, having assembled her workmen, she carefully chose her supply of provisions, materials and other necessities. When the castle was completed and her accounts made up, she discovered that all she was out of pocket was the sum of one groat (4d).

Postcard of Monkstown streetscape, *c.*1900 (source: Cork City Museum)

Other owners included Michael Boyle, the Archbishop of Armagh and a Lord Chancellor of Ireland. In the late eighteenth century, it was owned by Bernard Shaw. The initials 'BS' are carved into an immense stone chimneypiece, as well as the date 1636. It also served time as a military barracks, with 450 soldiers attached, while other owners included the Newenham family.

In 1908 Monkstown Golf Club was established by a number of residents, who formed themselves into a local development association and leased the lands of Monkstown Castle from Viscount de Vesci, at a nominal rent.

When the Viscount died, the club members were given a 'buy or get out' ultimatum by his trustees. The Monkstown members rallied to the challenge and, in 1959, purchased the land for a reasonable amount, the bulk of which they themselves contributed gratuitously.

Monkstown Castle served as its clubhouse until 1971. During that period it was occupied by catering and caretaking staff. When the golf club moved to new premises it was left to decay. Unfortunately, it was subjected to continuous vandalism during the following forty years. The structure was then bought by private owners and restored to its former glory. However, as of 2018, the castle was being sold on again and awaiting new owners.

Ringaskiddy Castle (Castle Warren)

One of the first full surveys of the castles around Cork Harbour was conducted and published by the Cork Historical and Archaeological Society in 1914–15. Amidst their research is the story of Barnahely Castle in Ringaskiddy. It was probably built by an immediate descendant of Anglo–Norman Miles de Cogan. Miles de Cogan, the first of the name, came probably from Cogan in Glamorganshire, and was one of the principal Anglo–Norman invaders in the late twelfth century.

From what remains of the present castle, from which the keep is a short distance apart, it appears to be of fifteenth- or sixteenth-century construction. The ruined structure still presents an imposing appearance. Built up against this old castle at its north-eastern side is the now equally dismantled mansion erected by a branch of the Warren family in 1796 – hence it got the name of Castle Warren.

In John Windele's *Historical and Descriptive Notices of the City of Cork and its Vicinity*, compiled in 1846, mention is made of an effigy to be seen over a doorway here supposed to be that of Miles or Richard de Cogan, one or other of whom was said to have been buried in the adjacent graveyard of Barnahely.

With the advent of the seventeenth century came the downfall of the de Cogans of Barnahely. In 1602, it was the property of the Goggin family. On 21 April 1602, Thomas Fitzwilliam Goggin had to give recognition in Cork in the Court of Gerald Comerford, 2nd Lord Justice of Munster. He owed the large sum of 500 shillings in debts.

Circa 1642, the remainder of the de Cogans were driven out of their lands, as was the case with so many other of County Cork's leading families at that period. The farm of Barnahely, being three plowlands, was settled upon John Cooke, one of the Cromwellian judges for Munster.

The next owner of the castle and lands was Robert Warren of Kinneigh, County Cork, a captain in Oliver Cromwell's army, who first came to Ireland in 1649, when about 25 years old. At the end of the military campaign he was granted lands to make up for arrears of pay for past services. The Warrens built their mansion against the old Barnahely Castle.

Prospect Villa, near Ringaskiddy village, was built by Thomas Warren, the third son of Sir Robert, the 1st Baronet, and his descendants held land in the vicinity of Ringaskiddy into the twentieth century. Colonel Warren, of Coolgrena, near Queenstown, was also one of the Warrens of Castle in 1851. In the mid-to-late nineteenth century, Robert Warren disposed of the castle and lands of Barnahely. He went with his family to reside at Moyview, Co. Sligo, where he died on 26 March 1876, his wife having pre-deceased him.

Wallingstown Castle

On the north side of the Lee, and about a mile to the south west of Little Island Railway Station, stands on the Bury estate the very small castle of Wallingstown. The Wallings were probably of the same family as John Waleys, Mayor of Cork in 1311. In 1553, this castle was held for a time by the Fitzgeralds. In the eighteenth year of Charles the Second's reign the lands of Sarsfieldstown, alias Wallingstown, were granted to Alexander Pigott.

3

FORTS AND FORTIFICATIONS

Camden Fort Meagher

It is difficult to imagine that in 2010 community volunteers had to cut their way into Camden Fort Meagher near Crosshaven. The scale of restoration work since then has been remarkable and is a testimony to the spirit and hard work of the whole project team. Passionate and imaginative are perhaps two key terms to describe the work of the community in their ongoing success in re-telling the story of the fort. There are multiple sides in their work, seeing its potential not just for the tourist market but also a way of bringing people together collaboratively and on rebuilding the fort's sense of place set against the spectacular backdrop of Cork Harbour.

Camden Fort Meagher is internationally recognised as being one of the finest remaining examples of a classical coastal artillery fort in the world. It combines a rich British and Irish military history. Fortifications on this site date back to 1550 and for almost 400 years the fort played an important role as a strong strategic position for the defence of Ireland, the west coast of England and Wales. However, most of what the visitor sees now was built during the 1860s by British forces and finished around 1871. It has been documented that it took 500 men forty years to carve out the moat, which goes around three sides of Camden Fort Meagher – as, of course, on the fourth side one has the harbour.

At the gate to the fort you can see the original pillars inscribed with 'Dun Ni Mhecair', which is the Irish for Fort Meagher. The fort was renamed Fort Meagher in 1938 after Thomas Francis Meagher, who was the leader of the Young Irelanders. Ninety years previously, in 1848, Meagher and fellow patriot William Smith O'Brien went to France to study revolutionary events there and returned with the new Flag of Ireland, a tricolour of green, white and orange, made by and given to them by French women sympathetic to the Irish cause.

A map reproduced for the visitor at the entrance to the fort was originally produced in 1896 by the royal engineer Lieutenant Colonel H. Kirkwood. The fort itself is 45 acres and the resources of the fort are 65 per cent underground. There are numerous gun emplacements that protected the fort on all sides. One of the most interesting facts about the fort is that it once housed one of only eight installations of the Brennan Torpedo worldwide. This was the world's first practical guided torpedo. Remains of a gun emplacement show that it housed a heavy mechanical gun and that would have had quite a long range. You can also see the remains of pulley bars that would have enabled the pulling and dragging of heavy guns by many men. The bulk of ammunition and shells relevant to each gun emplacement would have been kept directly underground in a magazine and store.

Further inside the fort, there are the casemated barracks where approximately 240 soldiers would have slept at one time. There were thirteen casemated barracks in peace time and twenty-two in war time. Some of these rooms have been imaginatively reused to house exhibitions covering the timelines of British and Irish history at the fort. One of these rooms houses seasonal international exhibitions.

The impressive tunnels, some of which are accessible, were built with a 'cut and cover' method, which meant that the workers would dig trenches in the ground, put up support structures, brick over that, then remove the support structures and then fill the earth back over the tunnel. The underground magazine is the biggest chamber in Camden Fort Meagher and was once a store for the fort's vast amounts of munitions, approximately 30ft underground. The acoustics in there are intense – this is due to the vaulted ceiling, which was designed to support the weight and stress of the Parade Square which lies above it. You can see the boxes at the gable end here are numbered 2, 3 and 4 – these were light boxes that were secured tightly with glass and putty and would have been lit from an access passage behind the magazine. This kept flames and sparks separate from the munitions, for obvious reasons.

The Parade Square at the centre of the fort dates from 1550 right up to 1989. Today, the Parade Square is used for re-enactments highlighting different eras and displays. In 1989, the Irish Army handed the fort over to the local authority, Cork County Council. Despite best efforts to restore the fort as a tourism site it was overgrown for almost two decades. Serious input by a community of volunteers, and financial and logistical support from the local authority Cork County Council, have been crucial to the development of this heritage site.

Fort Carlisle

Opposite Camden Fort Meagher is Fort Carlisle, renamed Fort Davis in time. It was constructed on the site of a seventeenth-century fort and atop the site of Rupert's Tower. The earliest fortification was named King John's Fort. Its hilly location was strategic in order to repel foreign fleets of ships with no permission to enter the inner harbour.

Rupert's Tower was a square building and may have been built by the Roches or by Prince Rupert. Rupert was the nephew of King Charles I, and spent some time with his cousin, Charles II, in Cork in 1649, After first putting into Crookhaven, County Cork, Prince Rupert next entered Kinsale Harbour soon after the execution of Charles I, with sixteen ships displaying black jacks, ensigns and pennants; the Prince and all his officers were in deep mourning. He came to prepare the way for Charles II.

The National Inventory of Architectural Heritage records that much of the present-day fort was built *c*.1800 and was an irregular-plan fortification. Fast forward to the 1860s, and the fort had twenty big guns guarding the mouth of the harbour. The enclosing deep fosse was constructed *c*.1870. Carlisle Fort and Fort Camden did

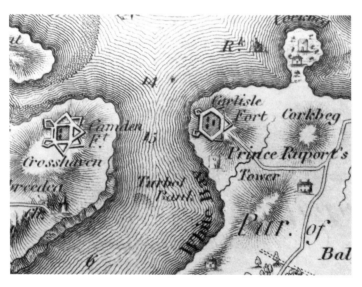

Forts Camden and Carlisle from Grand Jury Map of Cork, 1811 (source: Cork City Library)

not work in isolation. Both their promontories mirrored each other in their design.

The fort was named in honour of the Earl of Carlisle, who was appointed Lord Lieutenant in 1870. It was renamed Fort (Thomas) Davis when it was returned to the Irish government along with the other Treaty Ports in 1938. Mallow-born Thomas Davis (1814–45) was an Irish writer who was the chief organiser of the Young Ireland movement.

In October 2015, the Irish Defence Forces, which now operates Fort Davis, uncovered a 100m-long underground tunnel, part of a network beneath the complex. On clearing scrubland, they also discovered old ruins and pillboxes along with the remains of torpedo bays in the hewn-out rock at the bottom of the three-level structure, the majority of which is underground. The 1st Cavalry Squadron took three weeks to clear the 100m-long tunnel. Torpedo bays believed to date to the First World War were found. The squadron is also in charge of maintaining a graveyard on the site where a mix of British and Irish troop members are buried. The gravestones date from the different epochs in the fort's rich history.

Haulbowline by Robert Lowe Stopford, *c.*1850 (source: Cork City Library)

Coastguard Stations

In February 1804, in Cork Harbour the Sea Fencibles (Marine Yeomanry) were established for coastal defence. Their boats were divided into six divisions. However, by the conclusion of the Napoleonic Wars in 1815, over 300,000 soldiers and sailors were released. Due to unemployment and many other reasons, thousands turned to a life of smuggling. As a countermeasure, the Sea Fencibles across the UK were reorganised. The emerging Preventative Water Guard reported to the UK treasury. The suite of new ships was operated by the Admiralty and the riding officers were answerable to Customs.

Penny's Dock in Passage West was the location of a watch house serving the Preventative Water Guard Service. The Water Guard was the sea-based arm of revenue enforcement. Water Guard boat crews patrolled the coast each night to counteract smuggling. They were also tasked with the helping ships in trouble and with keeping plunderers off wrecked ships.

In 1829, The first coastguard instructions were published. It contained much information on how to deal with discipline but also outlined the many duties of a coastguard. For example, when informed of a shipwreck the coastguard was accountable to do as much as possible to save lives and save as much of an afflicted vessel. As a result of a further review of the service in 1831, it was decided that the coastguard should become a reserve force for the Royal Navy. It was not until the passing of the Merchant Shipping Act of 1854 that the government took the first formal steps to assume direct responsibilities for life saving at sea.

The creation of coastguard stations was an important addition to the work of the coastguard. From the decade of the 1830s, the coast of Ireland became dotted with such stations, especially where smuggling was probable. Some had defensible outer wall features. A comfortable cottage was provided to each man and his family. The officer on duty was given a larger house and a watch room. A total of fifty-six coastguard stations were created along the County Cork coastline in the early nineteenth century with eight within Cork Harbour. The Harbour locations included Cork City Port, Blackrock, Crosshaven, East Ferry, Queenstown, Spike Island, Whitegate, and at the mouth of the harbour Roche's Point, Myrtleville and Ringabella. All were self-contained living quarters. For example, in 1909, Mytleville had a chief boatman's house, three men's houses and gardens, and a boat house. Crosshaven is the only one to still host a lifeboat as part of the Royal National Lifeboat Institution.

A Tapestry of History at Haulbowline

After the Battle of Kinsale (1601) between the Irish and Spanish versus English forces, the weaknesses in the defence of Cork harbour became apparent. In 1602, at the highest point on the northern rise of Haulbowline a bastioned fort began. By 1624, military reports do not emphasise the fort. It had been abandoned. By 1665 it is said to have been a complete ruin. It did not play any part in the 1690 Williamite attack of Cork Harbour and City.

As far back as 1778, Haulbowline Island was little better than a rock standing out of the sea. The authorities of the time saw its advantages, and purchased it from the then Lord Inchiquin, and buildings were built upon it on at the instruction of the Board of Ordnance. At that point the famous old Cork Harbour Water Club, which had its meeting house on the highest point of Haulbowline, had to leave their surroundings and move to Queenstown.

The Martello tower was constructed in 1813–15 on the high ground at the northern edge of Haulbowline Island. Circa 1813, a barracks to accommodate three officers and sixty men, two storehouses, a gun carriage yard, smithy and carpenters' workshop and other installations were constructed. Circa 1820, on the naval side of the island (i.e. the eastern side), a large victualling yard containing six large storehouses, living quarters for the supply staff and medical officers, houses for the chief surgeon, the coopers, and other workshops were erected. The island was extended by 4.5 acres of reclaimed land in order to construct the flat wharfage area. The building contractor was Mrs Deane of Cork.

It took a long time for the British Admiralty to move on the actual construction of the dock. In 1855, it was begun. As Haulbowline was so close to Spike Island, convicts were sent to hew out rock and dig the deep foundations. The construction of a wooden bridge from Spike to Haulbowline was speedily undertaken, and brought to completion within one year, and thenceforward every morning prisoners, mostly handcuffed, could be seen walking their way to the scene of the present dockyard. Guarded en route by armed warders, when the day's work was done, the convicts were marched back over that same bridge.

On 11 July 1938, Haulbowline was handed back to the Irish Free State. On part of the island a steel plant was built to assist Cobh recover from the loss of income from the departing British forces. Since 1946, Haulbowline has been home to the Irish Naval Service. The navy is principally involved in fisheries protection, sea patrols, European humanitarian missions and smuggling prevention. Since 2008, the navy has intercepted €1.7 billion worth of drug shipments in Irish waters. In 2014 the Irish Government bought the €48 million ship LE *Samuel Beckett*. In a press release issued on the day, it denoted that it is the fastest ship in the Irish fleet and also boasts 'Star Wars' capabilities for Remotely Operated Aerial Vehicles (ROV drones) as well as robotic submersibles. Annually, the navy carries out over 400 vessel boardings.

The Magazine of Rocky Island

In 1810 on Rocky Island, which was a small rocky outcrop situated to the south of Haulbowline, a magazine was constructed. The island was originally conical and the east and west sides of the rock were excavated and large vaults placed beneath the levelled surface. The vaults were created to host 25,000 barrels of powder. Into these vaults two magazine buildings were built, of which only one survives. In August 1939, the Haulbowline Steel Syndicate started production of steel. In 1966, the company constructed a bridge allowing for easier access to Haulbowline from the mainland. After sixty-two years of production, the steel plant was closed in 2001. In February 2005, the Island Crematorium Co Ltd. bought Rocky Island and its magazine building, bringing new services to the general public.

Rocky Island, from Cork Camera Club archives, *c.*1900 (source: Cork City Museum)

Spike Island

In September 2017, Fortress Spike Island was named 'Europe's Leading Tourist Attraction' at the 2017 World Travel Awards 2017, seeing off a shortlist which included the Eiffel Tower, Buckingham Palace and the Coliseum. In December 2017, the Island finished second at the World Travel Awards 2017 in Vietnam, second only to Machu Picchu in the 'World's Leading Tourist Attraction' category. Walking through the Spike Island history experience, the different layers of time are articulated by numerous history panels animating the story of the 104-acre site.

There is some evidence that a monastery was founded on Spike Island (Inis Pic) in the seventh century AD. The well-known saint, St Mochuda or St Carthage, is said to have founded a monastery here in AD 635. Fast forward to the 1770s, during the turmoil of the American War of Independence, Cork Harbour replaced Kinsale as the principal Royal Navy base on the south coast. To strengthen the defences of the harbour, a decision was taken to build a fort on Spike Island. It was named Fort Westmoreland and was completed by 26 July 1779. In time, the British military quickly realised the strategic importance of Spike and decided to replace the old fort with a much larger structure. The British military surveyor General Charles Vallancey and architect Michael Shanahan were responsible for the new fort and the foundation stone was laid on 6 June 1804. It consisted of six bastions connected by ramparts and surrounded by a dry moat and outer artificial slopes.

Following an upsurge in crime during the Great Famine (1845–52), the fort was converted to a prison in 1847 as part of the British colonial government's response to the rise in public disorder. In its early years, it was an important holding centre for convicts transported to Australia and Bermuda. Political prisoners such as the Young Irelander, John Mitchel (after whom the fort is now named), and Fenians were also incarcerated on Spike. Originally devised as a temporary solution, it went on to operate as a prison for thirty-six years, holding up to 2,300 people at any one time in appalling, overcrowded conditions.

John Mitchel (1815–75) was an Irish nationalist activist, solicitor and political journalist. Born near Dungiven, Co Derry, he became a leading participant of both Young Ireland and the Irish confederation. He was an outspoken opponent of British rule and in 1843 he was convicted of sedition and sentenced to transportation to Bermuda for fourteen years. On 27 May 1848, Mitchel was sent from Dublin on board HMS *Scourge* to Spike Island, where he was incarcerated for three days. On Spike Island, Mitchel met Edward Walsh (1805–49), the noted poet and schoolmaster of the prison on the island. From Bermuda,

Mitchel was directed to the penal colony of Van Diemen's Land – now Tasmania. Arising from this journey he wrote his famous Jail Journal. Mitchel escaped from the colony in 1853 and settled in America. He returned to Ireland and was elected to the British House of Commons, only to be disqualified because he was a convicted felon. He died on 20 March 1875 in Newry. The Fort on Spike Island was renamed Fort Mitchel in his honour in 1961.

By 1883, a reduction in the overall number of prisoners led to the closure of the prison and it once again became a purely military complex. However, the island's days as a prison were not over. In 1916, the captured crew of the *Aud*, a ship carrying a cargo of arms for Ireland to aid the Easter Rising, was held on the island prior to being transferred to a POW camp in England. During the War of Independence, Spike was used as a prison and internment centre for members of the Irish Volunteers. Up to 500 prisoners were housed in blocks and in wooden huts. At the end of the First World War, Ireland's struggle for independence mounted in intensity and Spike again became a detention camp for political prisoners. Much to the embarrassment of the British authorities who regarded escape from the island prison as impossible, three internees absconded in broad daylight in a motor-launch manned by members of the Cobh IRA Company. In 1921, an escape through an excavated tunnel which led outside the barracks to a waiting boat ready to put off for the main land was a daring feat carried out successfully against great odds amidst sentry spotting and a stormy sea. The boat landed safely at Holy Ground, Cobh. Amongst the prisoners who had risked their lives in the thrilling bid for liberty were Maurice Twomey, Bill Quirke, Dick Barrett, Tom Crofts, Henry O'Mahony, OC of the prisoners, Patrick Buckley and Patrick Eady. The transfer of Spike to the Irish government took place on 11 July 1938. From 1972 until 1982 it was used as a military detention centre. By 1980, the first Naval Service recruits came to the island. In the ensuing five years up to four classes a year were enlisted. In 1985, the government decided to convert the fort into a prison and the order was given for the naval garrison to stand down.

In July 2010, a new phase in Spike Island's history began as the state, specifically the Department of Justice and Law Reform, officially handed control over to Cork County Council, thus ending over two centuries of institutional use. The county council entered into a contract with experienced tour operators to conduct walking tours of the island, accessed from Cobh by a licensed ferry operator. Cork County Council recognises that there is a pent up demand from people to visit Spike, including people who formerly lived on the

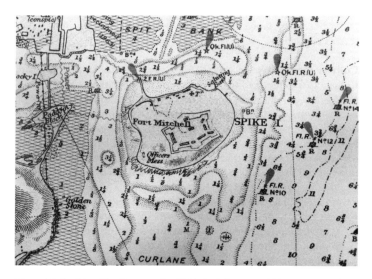

Map of Spike Island by Commander W. E. Archdeacon, 1888 (source: Cork City Library)

island. The county council has prepared medium- to long-term plans for the development of the island as a tourist attraction, including the integration of new uses for buildings both within and outside the star-shaped fort.

Notes from a Convict Prison

First arrival: On Saturday 9 October 1847, The *Minerva* steamer arrived from Dublin having on board 150 male convicts, destined for Spike Island, who were accompanied by a detachment of two sub-inspectors, three head constables, and seventy constables and sub-constables. The convicts were landed, and entrusted to the custody of Mr Grace, the acting governor.

A penal prison: By the end of 1847, The governor, Mr Grace (the now deputy-governor), twenty-five turnkeys, and two companies of soldiers received 600 prisoners sentenced to transportation. They were deployed first to making furniture and clothing for their own use, and the following year were set to work in raising a breakwater between the island and the Spit Back.

Resident provision: In 1847, it was intended to remove the fishermen and their families from the island on which they had resided for years, but a subsequent Government Order permitted their remaining under certain restrictions.

Convict mass grave: In July 2013, archaeologists from University College Cork identified for the first time the full extent of a convicts' mass grave on what was once a notorious concentration camp-style prison. Work by archaeologist Barra O'Donnabháin and his team unearthed records that revealed that over 1,100 convicts died on the island during its thirty-six years as a prison. He believes that more archaeological work will be required to uncover the full degree of the other burial sites, where a projected 900 or so convicts are buried.

Prison work: The convicts worked in gangs of eighteen, one warder to each gang. When the works on Forts Camden and Carlisle were completed the convicts were employed in excavating from the quarries in Haulbowline the huge stones used in the construction of the new government docks, built on the mud banks to the east of the island. To enable the convicts to reach Haulbowline from Spike, a causeway was constructed. In 2012 underwater archaeologist Niall Brady investigated offshore the east part of Haulbowline island – an area reclaimed from the Spit Bank. He discovered the underwater ruins of a causeway bridge that connected Haulbowline with Spike Island. The causeway bridge was encased in stonework, and from a painting of *c.*1870 Niall Brady suggested that it was originally founded on timber piles.

Convict badges: Each prisoner wore two badges. In the first badge P.S. stood for penal servitude. There was the prisoner's register number, and the number of years of penal servitude. In the second badge a number stood for the number of marks the prisoner had to make to rise from a third-class prisoner to second class. Further numbers signified marks for discipline, for good conduct, and for industry. Additional numbers signified that he had more marks to make up.

The Influences of Cape Martello

The name Martello originates from Cape Martello in Corsica where a circular tower of this type was first observed by the British Navy. It was captured with excessive effort in 1794 by British forces who were assisting Corsican revolutionaries against the French. Being impressed with the structure, in 1803 the Duke of York (as Commander-in-Chief) commended this type of tower for coastal defence in the UK. He was very concerned with the increasing threat to England of invasion by Napoleon Bonaparte. The plans with a complete model had been carefully transported back to England after the engagement at Corsica and consequently Martello Towers were built in the most vulnerable parts of the British and Irish coast. Many of them were round but a few were elliptical in shape, while the walls were about 1m thick and 10m in diameter. Entrance to the tower was about 12ft up and a stairway was cut into the inner wall on the side farthest from attack. Their plan consisted of two storeys; the basement containing the magazine and store rooms, and the upper storey forming a casement for the defender. Two or three gunners and their families lived in them. The towers each had a 12-pound gun which could rotate to counter an attack from any direction.

Altogether, 103 Martello Towers were built in Britain, most, naturally, near the site of the Dover-France Channel opening, and others were built in North America and South Africa. On the east coast of Ireland twelve such towers were built between Dublin and Balbriggan to the north, and sixteen between Bray and the south. On the west coast three were built south of Galway and one to the west. In all, seventy-four Martello Towers were built at a cost of £2,000 each, and that number included two built in Banagher, County Offaly. The first constructed in Cork being on Garnish Island, Glengarriff, in 1804 followed by four on Bere Island.

Five were constructed in the Cork Harbour area. Each was armed with one gun, which revolved upon the roof. They were placed at different points of the harbour, the lower river, and its inlets. Foaty Bay, on the north side of the river opposite Passage, has two of those towers; there is another one at Belvelly, commanding the bridge which connects the Great island with the mainland. Another stands on Haulbowline Island. The fifth stands at Ringaskiddy. Cork towers are slightly oval. The building of the tower at Fota Island was a major operation, as a quay had to be built in the foreshore. Youghal brick was transported there.

The Foaty Bay Tower was attacked by members of the Irish Republican Brotherhood on St Stephen's Night, 1867. William Lomassaney O'Connell from Passage West, whose ally was Captain Mackey, led the attack. The tower garrison consisted of two gunners of the Royal Artillery. With them, their two wives and five children occupied the tower. The entrance door of the tower was placed at some height from the ground, and was reached by means of a ladder, which was drawn up at dusk every evening. The country, for some distance around, was thinly populated, and the tower itself was located adjacent to the Cork Youghal Railway branch line to Queenstown.

The visitors took a number of 8-pound cartridges, variously stated from ten to twenty, besides a quantity of fuse, but did not find some cartridges that were hidden away as a reserve. After staying for some time, they left the tower, to which it is supposed they had come in boats. William Lomassaney was a man wanted by the police for the raid on the Martello Tower. He was arrested with two of his accomplices at Cronin's public house in Cornmarket Street, Cork, on 7 February 1868.

Signal Tower

The remains of a signal tower stand just east of Roche's Point lighthouse within the peninsula. It was one of eighty-one signal towers constructed around the Irish coast between 1804 to 1806. The British feared another invasion by France. The heaviest concentration was along the south coast. Signal Towers cost less than Martello Towers, about £600–£900. These were about 14ft square and the walls were usually about 2ft thick; slate work was a feature. The entrance was on the first floor, through a door on the front wall. As a rule they housed three signallers and had local Yeomen as guards. A much larger force manned the Martello Towers. They communicated with adjacent towers and with ships at sea, using the flag-and-ball signalling system. The system was mounted on a top-mast, similar to the main mast of a ship, using flags of different shapes and balls on a crossbeam made of hoops covered in canvas to transmit message by line of sight along the chain of towers to the authorities in Dublin. There was also a telescope, and around ten British military personnel would have lived in the two-storey structures. Many signal towers fell into disrepair and ruin after the Battle of Waterloo in 1815.

Templebreedy Fort

Templebreedy Fort was a coastal defence fortification close to Crosshaven. Supplementing a number of earlier structures at Fort Camden and Fort Davis, the site was developed between 1904 and 1909 to defend the mouth of Cork Harbour. Used as a coastal artillery position until the 1940s, and as a military training camp until the late twentieth century, many of the structures of the 37-acre site were dismantled over time, and part of the complex used as a pitch-and-putt course. In 2009, Cork County Council added the site to a proposed list of protected structures – though as of 2013 it remains in the ownership of the Department of Defence.

Adjacent the fort on top of a hill, overlooking the entrance to Cork Harbour, is an irregular-shaped graveyard enclosed by stone walls. There are many low uninscribed grave markers; the earliest inscribed headstone dates to 1711. There are forty eighteenth-century headstones. Near the southern end are the roofless ruins of the Church of Ireland church of St Matthew, which was erected in 1778, near the site of a former church.

4

JOURNEYS THROUGH COASTAL VILLAGES

WEST TO EAST

Delights of Douglas

Douglas village, which is situated at the head of a small bay called Douglas channel, on the western side of Cork harbour, was irregularly built in two detached portions on the upper and lower roads from Cork. The story of Douglas and its environs seems to be in part a story of experimentation, of industry and of people and social improvement. It possesses the story of one of Ireland's largest sailcloth factories. The ridges overlooking the industrious and growing village were home to forty or so seats or mansions and demesnes where the city's merchants made their home. Those landscapes that were created still linger in the environs of Douglas village.

The dark stream: The district of Douglas takes its names from the river or rivulet bearing the Gaelic word *Dubhghlas* or dark stream.

The King's proclamation: In an inquisition of the lands of Gerald de Prendergast in 1251, Douglas is first mentioned. In 1299, Douglas was one of the towns listed in County Cork wherein the King's proclamation was to be read out.

The Roche connection: In 1372, in an inspection of the dower of Johanna, widow of John de Rocheford, there is a reference to allotments of land to her in Douglas. The Roches originally came from Flanders, then emigrated to Pembrokeshire in Wales, before three of the family – David, Adam and Henry de la Roch – joined Strongbow in the Anglo–Norman invasion of Ireland in the twelfth century. In all, there are sixteen Rochestowns in Ireland and innumerable Roche castles.

The Huguenot sailcloth factory: On 1 June 1726, the construction of Douglas Factory was begun. Huguenot members Samuel Perry and Francis Carleton were the first proprietors. They were also members of the Corporation of Cork. The eighteenth century was the last golden age for wooden sailing ships, before the 1800s made steam and iron prerequisites for modern navies and trading fleets. It was a golden age too for maritime exploration, with the voyages of James Cook, amongst others, opening up the Pacific and the South Seas.

Worthy of notice: Robert Stephenson, a technical expert on the linen industry, visited every linen factory in the provinces of Munster, Leinster and Connaught. He visited Cork on 9 August 1755, saying: 'Near this city and in it are carried on the only sail cloth manufacturers worth notice at present in the Kingdom; Douglas Factory, the property of Messrs Perry, Carelton and Co. contains about 100 looms, with Boylers, Cesterns, Kieves and every apparatus for preparing the yarn to that number.'

St Luke's Church: On 21 July 1784, the Corporation of Cork granted £50 to Messrs John Shaw (sailcloth manufacturer), Jasper Lucas (gentlemen), Aylmer Allen (merchant) and Julius Besnard towards the new St Luke's church, provided that 'a seat shall be erected in said Church for the use of the Corporation'.

Douglas Fingerpost: The original 15ft-high wooden Douglas Fingerpost was located at the junction of the Maryborough and Rochestown Roads. It was supported at the base in a beehive-shaped pile of stone. Local folklore denotes that a local man, Phil Carty of Donnybrook, is said to have been hanged on the original Fingerpost for his part in the 1798 Rebellion and his corpse left lifeless in chains there. For decades after, people passing blessed themselves. Still an iconic structure, the twentieth century replacement commands the busy traffic of a bustling village.

Roman Catholic Church: Historically, Douglas was part of Carrigaline parish until 1750, when the first local parish church was erected near Grange Cross. The penal laws, which prohibited Catholic worship, had been sufficiently relaxed to allow open practice of the Catholic faith. The present church was built in 1814, over a decade before Catholic Emancipation.

The largest ropeworks: In 1863, Wallis and Pollock's Douglas Patent Hemp Spinning Company were the largest ropeworks in the south of Ireland, which had been established within the former Douglas sailcloth factory, erected scotching machinery.

A new mill: The surviving multi-storey flax-spinning mill at Donnybrook was designed and built by the Cork architect and antiquarian Richard Bolt Brash for Hugh and James Wheeler Pollock in 1866. Its essential design, like that of the Millfield flax-spinning mill, was modelled closely on contemporary Belfast mills.

Company-owned cottages: In 1889, the mill was bought by James and Patrick Morrough and R.A. Atkins, the High Sheriff of Cork. In 1903, the mill employed 300 people, many of whom were housed in the 100 company-owned cottages in Douglas.

O'Brien's Mills: In 1883, the O'Brien Brothers built St Patrick's Mills in Douglas Village. It was designed by a Glasgow architect. O'Brien's Mills were extended in the closing decades of the nineteenth century, and by 1903 operated with some eighty looms and employed 300 workers, many of whom lived in company-owned houses in Douglas village.

The future of shopping: In the late 1960s, Jim Barry (of Kelly & Barry & Associates) designed the Douglas shopping centre with a design typical of the period with an open and uncovered mall.

Some Stories of Big Houses

Ronayne's Court: It was built by wealthy wine merchants connected with the Court of Spain. The inscription on the fire place says 'Morris Ronayne and Margaret Gould built this house in the years of Our Lord, 1627 and in the third yeare of King Charles'. The fireplace is now on display in Blackrock Castle. The house was demolished in 1969.

Monfields House: The twenty-eight-roomed Monfieldstown House was once the residence of the Kearney family. Local historian Con Foley tells that sometime in the early 1800s the house was the location of a tragic wedding party story. The bridal party had just returned from the church and the guests sat around the breakfast table waited patiently for the bride and groom to cut the wedding cake. Unexpectantly, a horseman rode rapidly up the coach driveway to the house, and charged into the house. It was the bride's former suitor, returning now with his wealth made, to claim her hand in marriage. Angrily he gave out to her for not waiting and marrying another man. In an act of repentance, the girl pulled out a diamond pin – the gift of her groom – and fatally stabbed herself.

Another telling of the story suggests that she was on the point of cutting the wedding cake and that she plunged the knife into her heart.

The guests rushed quickly from the scene with the wedding food left on the table uneaten. Years later, it is said that when the carpet was lifted, a brown bloodied stain could still be viewed on the floorboards.

It is reputed that Dickens immortalised that tragedy in *Great Expectations*, published in serial form in 1861. Dickens had given a reading of his works in the Athenaeum (now the Cork Opera House) and, during his visit to Cork, stayed in a house near Donnybrook Mill.

Windsor House: Standing on the Rochestown Road, Windsor House was owned for generations by Lord Bandon and his predecessors. In the mid-nineteenth century, it was purchased by Sir Abraham Sutton, a covert of the Fr Theobald Mathew Temperance campaign, and colleague of Daniel O'Connell in his struggle for Catholic Emancipation. In time, the house came into the possession of the Kiltegan Fathers and now forms part of the foyer area of the Rochestown Park Hotel.

Maryborough House: Now an exquisite hotel, it was built in 1720–30 with a 370-acre estate surrounding it. It was the residence of Richard Newenham, who owned the banking company of Newenham and Company.

Frankfield House: The Landed Estate database records that Frankfield House was once the residence of Samuel Lane in 1837, a famous Cork brewer, and of Reverend H.J. Newman in the mid-nineteenth century. The house is located on the site of what is now the Frankfield Golf Club.

Vernon Mount: Built by Atwell Hayes, he had commercial interests in brewing, milling and glass-making, the latter being the Cork Glasshouse Company located in Hanover Street, which occupied part of the Beamish & Crawford Brewery. The house, now an unfortunate burnt-out ruin, was originally designed by Abraham Hargrave, an English architect. The house was named Vernon Mount, commemorating the ancestral home of George Washington. The renowned artist Nathaniel Grogan was commissioned to carry out ceiling and door paintings based on figures from classical mythology. A severe fire in July 2016 reduced the structure to a largely empty shell.

Sir Henry Hayes is better known though for his abduction activity three years after the death of his wife. He attempted to forcibly marry Mary Pike. Mary had inherited a substantial fortune from her father Samuel Pike, who was a prominent banker and who lived in Bessborough House. Sir Henry was captured by the local police for his crime. He was sentenced to death at the Cork Assizes in 1801. He successfully asked the judge to be granted a reduction of his sentence and was commuted to deportation to New South Wales.

Curiosities of Carrigaline

Carrigaline is part of the ancient Irish territory of Ciarridhe-Cuirrche, which has since become the present barony of Kerricurrihy. This district must have been intensely populated from a very early period, as every townland in it is studded with ringfort earthworks variously known as 'rath', 'dun', and 'lios'. Carrigaline in early times was called *Beavor*, or *Bebhor*, and derived its name from the abrupt rocky cliff on which are the remains of the ancient castle. It was built by Miles de Cogan and for nearly two centuries occupied by the Earls of Desmond. By the nineteenth century, the village consisted of several houses and cottages, extending into the parish of Kilmoney, on the south side of the river, over which is a bridge of three arches.

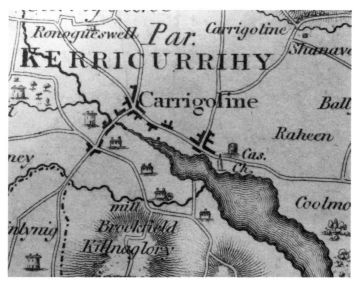

Carrigaline village, from *Grand Jury Map of Cork*, 1811 (source: Cork City Library)

The Church of the Clerics: The first recorded church in Carrigaline was Cill na gClearach, the Church of the Clerics, from which the townland of Kilnagleary derives its name. This church dated from the seventh century AD and the monks who founded it were most likely associated with St Finbarr's monastery in Cork.

An elegant space: Samuel Lewis in his Topographical Dictionary of Ireland highlights that in 1823, St Mary's Church of Ireland Carrigaline was constructed:

> It is composed of hewn limestone, with a large square tower crowned with pinnacles and surmounted by an elegant and lofty octagonal spire pierced with lights. It was near the site of the former church, and enlarged in 1835 by the addition of a north transepts.

Near the west front Samuel Lewis describes a lofty arch beneath which is an altar-tomb of grey marble, with a damaged 'recumbent leaden figure' of Lady Susanna Newenham, who died in 1754.

Village fairs: In 1837, fairs were held in Carrigaline on Easter Monday, Whit Monday, 12 August, and 8 November for cattle, sheep, and pigs. There was a penny post to Cork, and a chief constabulary police force stationed here. Petty sessions were held in the courthouse every Tuesday, and a manorial court once in three weeks.

Milling traditions: Milling in Carrigaline can be traced back to 1760 when Michael Roberts established the first flourmill at Kilmoney Glen. In 1837, there were two large boulting mills, the property of Messrs Michael Roberts and Company, which ground 12,000 sacks of flour annually, of which the greater part was shipped for England from Cork. The trade comprised chiefly the export of corn, flour, and potatoes, and the import of coal and culm. The channel of the river was deepened and vessels could deliver their cargoes at the bridge. The mill closed later in the nineteenth century.

The Centenary Garden: By the early 1930s, Carrigaline resident John Cogan had built up a considerable flour mill business meeting the needs of the Carrigaline area and further afield. During the emergency years his mill was in constant demand and he provided a great service to the community during a time of scarcity in that he produced a wide range of milled products including flour, bran, crushed oats, etc. He continued the milling business up to the early 1970s, at which time he retired. In 1980, his residence and farm together with the mill were demolished to make way for the housing development known today as Millwood, and in 2016 Carrigaline Tidy Towns added to the site by creating a 1916 Irish Easter Rising commemorative garden.

Carrigaline Pottery: In 1930, the initiative in the establishing of a pottery industry in the district was led by Mr H.W.B. Roberts of Carrigaline. Mr D.L. Daly, managing director of the well-known firm of M.D. Daly and Co, Ltd, Academy Street, Cork, was chairman. The other directors were Captain T.A. Clarke, Messrs J.J. Horgan and A.W. Cooke. Two years earlier, in 1928, Captain Clarke sent a sample of local clay to North Staffordshire Pottery College, Stoke-on-Trent, for analysis. Mr L.T. Keeling, the manager of the Carrigaline Potteries since their establishment, was then in the college, and he made the necessary tests. Mr Keeling made a teapot from the clay sent by Mr Hodder Walworth Blacker Roberts. The pottery began in a ruined flour mill with an improvised workshop and one kiln and its staff of six began to make teapots, which enjoyed instant success on the home market. The pottery products became famous for their beauty and durability.

In 1934, a second oven was installed, but the native demand for their products became so great that further expansion became necessary. The expansion meant the enlarging of the premises to approximately ten times their original size. The most up-to-date type of machinery was installed and the range of products vastly enlarged. In just a few years, the company produced a wide range of items which were sold in many countries. In its early days, the finished product was brought by handcart to Carrigaline Railway Station. The main supply of brown clay was from Young's farm at Ballinrea. At first the local brown clay was used but when the firm went into mass production, white clay from Cornwall had to be utilised.

In 1979, the factory was taken over by a German, Lutz Kiel, who saved the factory from receivership and changed the name to the Cork Art Pottery, but within a couple of years was facing another financial crisis. The workers then took it upon themselves to save their jobs and the fortunes of the company when they bought the factory in 1983 and formed their own Co-op. By 1989, a Brazilian company had taken over, followed by the Stephen Pearce Pottery group based in Shanagarry in the mid-1990s. With the fall-off of a number of sectors, including tourism, and lower market share due to cheaper imports, the pottery workforce dwindled rapidly, with the factory ceasing production in 2003.

Carrigaline Pipe Band: The band had its origins during the Second World War in the Local Defence Force (LDF) in 1946, and initially performed in dyed RAF jackets obtained by Tom Morgan. It was not until two years later that it acquired proper uniforms and had its first parade in the village on Easter Sunday, 1948, a feast day which has always been special for the members.

The band has a proud history, winning ten Munster championships in a row in the 1950s and 1960s and the All-Ireland intermediate title in 1962. It had further successes with the drum corps in the early 1970s, as well as officiating at many important civic and sporting events. Following a number of years of hard work, the present band room at Church Road was opened in 1976.

Highlights over the decades included playing outside the then Provincial Bank next to Parnell Bridge when US President John F. Kennedy visited Cork in 1963, starring in the success of Carrigaline Pottery on TV in Tops of the Town in 1978, the twinning ceremony with Guidel in Brittany, and the visit of President Patrick Hillary for the opening of Carrigaline Community Complex in 1986. More recently, Carrigaline Pipe Band performed at the hosting of the Liechtenstein Special Olympics team in 2003, and in the 2005 International Folk Dance Festival which formed part of Cork European Capital of Culture year.

The Crystal Ballroom: The village hall was originally built as part of a flax mill, which was established in Carrigaline in 1919. The opening of the Assembly Hall was a great boon to the locality and it was availed of by many local organisations. Its size was ideal for sport as well as dancing, concerts etc., and for many years was used extensively by the badminton club. One of the bands to play the hall in Carrigaline in the Swingin' Sixties was The Dixies. The building had elaborate decoration and lighting and further renovations also included a magnificent maple floor, ceiling, mirrors and, of course, the crystal ball in the middle. In the years before the Majorca ballroom in Crosshaven, Reidy's 'Crystal' in Carrigaline was the place for dance-goers. Increased competition from purpose-built ballrooms and other factors resulted in the Crystal Ballroom being sold in the mid-1960s. The building was purchased by the parish and it became known as the Parish Hall.

Roman Catholic church: Local historian Seán O'Mahony outlines that the Chapel of St John the Baptist on Church Hill was first built in 1796. It was the key local place of worship for the people of Carrigaline until the opening of the Church of Our Lady and St John in 1957. In the 1920s, the Canty family had presented the site for a new church to the parish.

The Bishop of Cork, Cornelius Lucey, turned the first sod of the new site for the Church of Our Lady and St John on the Feast of the Annunciation in March 1955. The Church of Our Lady and St John cost £55,000. Work commenced in May 1955 and the church was completed by blessed and officially opened on 16 June 1957. The *Cork Examiner*, in previewing the opening of the church, highlighted the efforts of the local people. Before the work on building the new church had begun the collection from the local people had passed the £7,000 mark. The Diocesan central fund contributed £13,000, local fundraising efforts totalled £20,000 and the Edward Geary bequest in 1918 had grown in value to £19,000, all of which meant that the debt was cleared within one year. Four carved stone panels depicting the evangelists are outside the entrance of the church. They are signed by Cork sculptor Seamus Murphy. The church, in aid of different charities every year, hosts guest singers and guest choirs.

Community Centre: A little piece of legal history took place on 25 January 1990, when the former railway station was used for the very last time as a venue for the District Court. The court was to be held in the modern Community Centre off Church Road.

The Wren tradition: Every year, the Wren Day, or Lá an Dreoilín, takes place on Main Street, Carrigaline on St Stephen's Day. Every year, up to eighty-five people dress up. For over twenty-five years, the Carrigaline Wren Boys Street Carnival has been entertaining the public. The revival of the ancient tradition took place over twenty-five years ago when local man Barry Cogan and his family and friends championed its return.

Embedded in Celtic mythology, the Wren Day is said to be an old Samhain sacrifice or druidic ritual, much like Halloween. The wren, recognised for its winter song, represented the end of the year, or the year past. The word for 'wren' in Irish is *dreolín*, which could originate from the words *draoi* and *éan*, meaning 'druid bird'.

The Wren tradition or performance sees the Wren Boys chase and stone a (nowadays fake) winged winter creature. They then bind him to the uppermost part of a pole, which the leader conveys and parades through the village with traditional Irish céilí music. They would also go door-to-door, asking a penny for the wren's funeral.

If a contribution is not made, homeowners would run the risk of bad luck as the Wren Boys could bury the bird outside their house. Payment offered good luck and the giving of a wren feather to the householder.

Ancient stories relate that that it was a wren which warned the Jews where St Stephen was hiding, leading to his apprehension and demise by stoning. There is also an old Irish legend that when Oliver Cromwell's soldiers were asleep, and the Irish were about to attack, a flock of wrens rose into the air to wake Cromwell's forces with the beating of their wings.

The Wren Boys then continue the chase through pubs and the hotel, where they sing, play and dance as they go, and a collection is taken in aid of charities

The South Union Hunt also holds its annual Carrigaline Meet on St Stephen's Day and leaves the Strand Road car park on horseback.

La Beau Voir: It was Carrigaline Tidy Towns which campaigned to transform a very busy public square, which is one of the focal points in the town on Southside of Owenabue Bridge, into a state-of-the-art plaza of polished limestone. The plaza is landscaped with attractive ornamental trees and a plinth with a riverbank-themed sculpture of an otter. The otter sculpture is also known as *La Beau Voir et La Loutre* (or translated 'The Beautiful View and The Otter') hinting at the French/Norman origins of the town. The Otter is a well-known resident of the Owenabue River. The plaza was built by the Pavillion Garden Centre, Ballygarvan, and the Otter was created by local artist Peadar Drinan. Cork County Council provided valuable assistance on the project.

Corners of Crosshaven

Crosshaven village, as people know it today, is situated on an estuary to which it gives its name, but which is more generally known as the River Carrigaline. A large cross used to stand on the hill near the ruined St Matthew's Church of Templebreedy, which overlooks Church Bay. This cross was of such great height that it was a well-known guide to mariners. It is from this ancient cross that the village of Crosshaven got its name.

The Hayes intervention: On 21 April 1656, Captain Peyton le Hunte (brother to Colonel le Hunte, captain of Oliver Cromwell's bodyguard) assigned the townlands of Knocknagore and Ballinaneening to Richard Hayes of the city of Cork, gentleman, who paid £247 10*s* for the assignment.

Crosshaven House: In 1769, William Hayes undertook the building of the present Crosshaven House, a handsome limestone structure. Presumably, the old house was then demolished. Built in the Palladian style, this fine-cut limestone ashlar building has a three-storey central block with two detached pavilions to the east and west. Although the house was built in 1750, it remained unoccupied until the early nineteenth century so all joinery and decorative features date from after 1800. Thomas Hayes of Crosshaven was the owner of almost 1,600 acres in county Cork in the 1870s. Over 1,000 acres of his estate in the baronies of Kinalea and Kerrycurrihy were offered for sale in the Landed Estates Court in October 1872. It remained in the ownership of the Hayes family until the 1960s. Crosshaven House was sold by Colonel Pierce Hayes to an American, Graham Flint, in the late 1960s. In the mid-1970s the latter sold it to Crosshaven Development Committee, which converted the building into a community centre. In recent years the house was meticulously restored to its former glory and is open to the public. Spacious and elegant reception rooms are complemented by the five separate suites on the upper floors. The space also caters equally well for wedding parties, corporate events or private hire.

The coastguard station: Crosshaven village grew rapidly in the late eighteenth and early nineteenth centuries. One cause of growth was the construction in the mid-eighteenth century of houses for revenue officers or coastguards, whose responsibility was to prevent smuggling. It became popular for many family members in the area to serve a term in the navy before coming home to marry and settle down.

Fishery trade: An extensive fishery trade existed in the early nineteenth century but declined due to the high price of food during the Napoleonic wars. By 1910, small boats with oars, as seen in the postcard, were used by the men of Fountainstown, Myrtleville and Fennell's Bay. The fishing grounds were located around the harbour mouth. Those without boats waited for the mackerel to come inshore and caught them by the hundreds with large pocket nets. A barrel of salted mackerel could be seen in every fisherman's cottage in preparation for winter each year.

Crosshaven Roman Catholic Church: The foundation stone was laid in 1869. It is named after the patron saint of Crosshaven, John, as was the original Teampall Bríde. This Gothic-style church was commissioned by Canon Denis McSwiney and designed by Edward Welby Pugin, and is constructed of Little Island limestone. The builder was Richard Evans of Cork. The belfry is a later addition.

Holy Trinity Church: It was designed by the world-renowned ecclesiastical architect William Burges who also designed the 'mother church' of the Diocese of Cork, Saint Finbarre's Cathedral.

A century ago: A hundred years ago Crosshaven village comprised about 100 houses, which were small but well built. It also had one of the eight coastguard stations in the district of Queenstown. Several handsome villas and lodges closely adjoined the village and these were the summer residences of those who visited the coast for sea bathing. Crosshaven Village, in 1914, could boast a post, money order and telegraph office. Transport was by train to Cork, with trains every hour. There was also transport by steam to Queenstown and Monkstown. A growing tourism town, it had five hotels, twelve shopkeepers and four vintners. While many of these hotels and pubs have not survived into the present day, the modern village is regularly visited by Corkonians and visitors who indulge in its great pubs and renowned food.

First World War defences: In August 1914, a large number of troops were assembled to defend the entrance to Cork Harbour. Besides the full complement within the harbour forts, there were nearly 2,000 men scattered along the cliffs towards the west. The men on outpost duty comprised strong detachments from the 2nd Leinster Regiment stationed at Cork, the North Stafford from Buttevant, and the Royal Fusiliers from Fermoy.

Railway closure: In May 1932, it was officially announced that on and from 1 June all trains on the Cork, Blackrock, and Passage Railway between Crosshaven and Monkstown in both directions would cease to run. The train service between these points had been, up to some years previously, the main artery of holiday traffic to the popular seaside resort, which it linked to the city. The vast increase in the number of privately owned cars was responsible for a gradual but very noticeable falling off in the passenger service. The advent of the buses was virtually the death blow to the railway, which had functioned between Crosshaven and Cork for over thirty years.

Royal Cork Yacht Club: First located in what was known as Cove, now Cobh, the club is the oldest yacht club in the world, being founded in 1720. Much is written on the club based on its rich archival material by historian Alicia St Leger. The original club became defunct in 1765 but was re-established in 1802. In 1872, the Munster Model Yacht Club was established as a Corinthian Yacht Club to offer amateur racing rather than racing for wagers on yachts of wealthy owners. It changed its name and dropped the word 'Model' and became known as the Cork Harbour Yacht Club. Later in the decade it let go the word 'Harbour' and became the Cork Yacht Club. In 1831, the club received a royal charter from King William IV, and became the Royal Cork Yacht Club. In 1966 another entity, the Royal Munster Yacht Club, amalgamated with it to become as it is known today, the Royal Cork Yacht Club incorporating The Royal Munster Yacht Club. A new premises was opened in Crosshaven in 1957 (see Chapter 10, *Recreation and Tourism*).

Crosshaven boatyard: This well-known Irish boatyard was founded in 1957. Redevelopment was announced in April 1979 when the construction of a marina was proposed, which was to have accommodation for 120 yachts and motor boats up to 80ft long, and was to be the first commercial marina in Ireland. Designers of the project were the British firm Walcon, one of the leading marina developers in Europe. The marina is located adjacent to Crosshaven Boatyard on what was formerly slobland. The boatyard most famously built explorer Tim Severin's leather boat, which re-enacted the voyage of St Brendan from Ireland to Newfoundland in 1976-77 (see Chapter 8, *Tales of Shipping*).

The Majorca: The Majorca Ballroom in Crosshaven was a very popular musical Mecca in the 1960s and early '70s. Near to thirty Coras Iompair Éireann double-decker buses would transport revellers to the seaside village from Cork City. All sought the fast beat of the showband era (see Chapter 10, *Recreation and Tourism*).

The Merries: The village is known in the region for its season of amusements more affectionately known as 'The Merries', which has been operated by the Piper family for generations (see Chapter 6, *People, Place and Curiosities*).

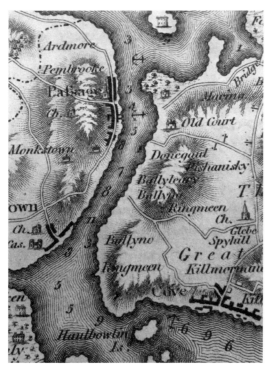

Passage West, from *Grand Jury Map of Cork*, 1811 (source: Cork City Library)

The Passage West

In the nineteenth century a dock and shipyard was founded in Passage West. Many merchants who depended on the River Lee and the Harbour Region for their livelihoods became shipowners, and carried on an extensive trade in their own vessels. Three of these individuals became well-known entrepreneurs: William Parker (who engaged in foreign speculation in shipping) and Thomas Parsons Boland and the Brown family. All offered invaluable employment to the people of Passage West and much further afield in the region. Numerous workers are recording boarding the Cork Blackrock and Passage Railway at Cork to come to the dockyard in Passage West.

The first Marmullane Church: It was built in the thirteenth or fourteenth century, and had become a ruin by 1615, but the graveyard of the ancient church continued to be used. It has some of the oldest graves in and around Cork Harbour. Local shipwright skills are reflected in both iron and rare timber grave markers.

Roman Catholic Church: There was a Roman Catholic church at the base of Church Hill from the 1740s. The present church, St Mary's, was built in 1791. By 1825, the structure had become dangerous and the church was closed. The walls were shored up to support the roof, and its reconstruction was funded entirely from local contributions. Rebuilding finished in 1832. Originally, access to St Mary's Church was through Lower Chapel Lane off Back Street. In the 1880s, some buildings in Chapel Square were demolished and new access to the church was opened. Lower Chapel Lane is now gone but the old bricked-up entrance to the church can still be seen in its boundary wall.

Streetscape: In 1837, writer Samuel Lewis detailed the town comprised one principal street, nearly a mile long, extending along the shore, and intersected by several smaller streets and lanes, which were mostly in a very rundown state. It contained 311 houses, of which 165 were in the parish of Monkstown, and the remainder in that of Marmullane. There was the parish church of Marmullane, a Wesleyan Methodist meeting house, the Roman Catholic chapel erected in 1832, two schools, and a dispensary. Petty sessions were held every Friday, and there was a constabulary police station.

Passage West ferries: From the eighteenth century to the decade of the 1870s, Passage West was the port of Cork. The channel upstream of Passage was not dredged and virtually all ships called to the town. One of only two ferries in the harbour serving Great Island operated out of

Passage West. All mail destined for Cobh went through Passage West and over to the Great Island on this ferry. In the nineteenth century, ferries up and down the river became a very popular way to travel from the lower harbour towns to Cork City. The first and most famous of these paddle steamer ferries was built by Hennessy's boatyard on the site of what is now Fr O'Flynn Park (named after the famous Cork City drama teacher of Shakespeare). She was launched from Passage West in 1815. The following year, the same Passage West boatyard launched the first paddle steamer manufactured completely in Ireland. The current Cross River Ferry between Glenbrook and Carrigaloe on Great Island opened in early March 1993.

The Steampacket Quay: It opened in 1836 and was designed by brothers George and Richard Pain, who designed Dromoland Castle and Mitchelstown Castle. It was the first quay built on this side of Cork Harbour. Before Steampacket Quay, all passengers and cargo arriving in Cork Harbour were discharged to the shore via rowing boat.

Royal Victoria Dockyard: In 1849, when Queen Victoria was visiting Cork Harbour, the Browns were given official permission to name their concern the Royal Victoria Dockyard. The Royal Victoria Dockyard was described as the 'most spirited and extensive undertaking probably ever attempted in Ireland by individual enterprise'. Established in 1832, twenty years later it comprised two dry docks, employed over 300 people who ran sailing and rigging lofts, workshops, stores, a steam sawmill and repaired up to 200 ships a year. Much employment was also afforded to labourers involved in discharging cargoes of all large vessels bound for Cork. The river up to Cork was not navigable for those above 400 or 500 tons' burden. By the 1870s, staff had increased to 700 and a four-storey granary was built on the site. With the dredging of the river of Cork and the demise of timber ships, the fortunes of the dockyard began to decline towards the end of the nineteenth century. It struggled on until 1931, when the plant and equipment were auctioned off.

The Woodlands Barge: Few construction works at Passage caused more interest than the building in 1877 of a large timber barque christened the *Woodlands* after the Montenotte residence of Sir John Arnott, the then chairman of the dockyard company. The reason for the great interest was that she was the first vessel to be built in Cork for a dozen years. She measured 150ft long, 27ft broad and 18ft deep. The barque was classed A1 at Lloyds for thirteen years, the highest class a wooden vessel could receive. Unfortunately, she perished on 15 April 1881 while bringing corn from New York to Gloucester. The crew were saved but the loss of the vessel, put at £3,500, and cargo (£3,000) was the subject of a lengthy Board of Trade inquiry.

The big house culture: During the nineteenth century, many merchants in Passage West built their own big houses and terraces. The Buildings of Ireland project records that Ardmore House was a detached five-bay, three-storey house, built *c.*1780 by the Roberts family. Rockenham is a detached irregular-plan, five-bay, two-storey country house, built *c.*1820 by the Johnson family. Horse Head is a fine Tudor Revival villa, which was built for John Craig in 1836, the Bank of Ireland's Cork agent. It was designed by Sir Thomas and Kearns Deane.

A bustling port: During the summers of the mid-nineteenth century, the town was much visited for its 'fine air and sea-bathing', with salt water baths open in nearby Glenbrook. The town recorded upwards of 100 covered cars, called jingles, engaged almost daily in the transport of people between Passage and Cork. Travelling between Cork and Passage several times daily carrying passengers on the river were steamboats and many small boats. Before Victoria Terrace (formerly known as Mariner's Row) was built, in the early nineteenth century the site was a fair field. Every summer a popular event called 'The Donnybrook of Cork' was hosted, at which events such as horse racing and boat races were carried out.

Memories of Monkstown

The name Monkstown came from the small establishment of Benedictine monks who lived at the now gone Legan Abbey. The monks belonged to the priory of St John's, Waterford. They formed a branch in Cork Harbour in the fourteenth century on a grant of land made to the original establishment by the family of McCarthy. In 1636 an Elizabethan-style house 'Monkstown Castle' was built on the side of a glen by Anastasia Archdeacon (see Archaeology, Antiquities and Ancient Towers section).

Anchorage: In the nineteenth century, the River Lee at Monkstown afforded every facility for water carriage, and there was excellent anchorage for vessels of all sizes as well as one of the connecting steamers to Cobh from the Cork Blackrock and Passage Railway Line.

St John Church of Ireland: Constructed in 1832, it was designed by well-known Cork architect William Hill and dedicated to St John the Evangelist. The Buildings of Ireland project relates that the design of the church follows that of the 'Early English style with characteristic tall and narrow lancets, buttresses, finely carved pinnacles and steeply pitched roofs'.

Church of the Most Sacred Hearts of Jesus and Mary, Chapel Hill: In 1862, this E.W. Pugin & George Ashlin-designed church was commissioned by local Canon William O'Connor. The canon had leased a plot of land on the side of Fairy Hill. The church is built with brown sandstone from Glanmire. Fr Henry Neville, parish priest from 1867, was in charge of overseeing the construction of the church and adjacent presbytery through to completion in 1872. The stained-glass window over the main door was by Francis Barrett of Edinburgh. The Gothic Revival Roman Catholic church was completed in 1872.

General depression: In 1875, a general depression within the shipping trade hit the local dockyards. In 1900, there was talk of the international ship construction firm of Harland and Wolfe coming to Monkstown and, although there was much enthusiasm for the project, it never materialised. The Royal Victoria Dockyard in Passage West began a policy of salvaging and reconstructing vessels. For a time, this was successful. Monkstown Golf Club was set up in 1908 in an attempt to attract some of the railway passengers to the area. By the summer of 1909, thirteen return trains were running on weekdays between Cork and Monkstown. However, the train service ran at a loss.

Cork Harbour Marina: A yacht club was first formed in Monkstown in 1870. A sailing club and rowing club regularly takes part in local and national competitions. In addition, presently Cork Harbour Marina is a ninety-berth facility. Publicly displayed plans for phase two will increase the marina's capacity to 280 berths.

Present Day: Today, Monkstown is now well known for its marina and popular and award-winning restaurants such as the Bosun run by the Moynihan family. The pub walls display a series of prints, some depicting scenes of local interest, including a historic picture of the old Cork–Crosshaven railway line. Photographs of the *Asgard II* and the world-famous Cunard liner the *QE2* add to the pub's maritime theme.

The Vale of Glanmire

Glanmire (*Gleann Maghair*) literally means 'The valley of the small fish', the valley of the ploughed land, the 'still vale' or the 'valley of the young fish'. The village of Glanmire is situated on both sides of the meandering river Glashaboy, which feeds into the north-west part of Cork Harbour. The well-known triple-arch humpback road bridge was built *c*.1790.

Mills: In the early nineteenth century there were extensive flour mills belonging to Mr Shaw, and in the surrounding area were those of Messrs Thorley and Son, for finishing calico and linen, and Mr Lyons and Hanly's woollen factory.

The Church of Ireland: St Mary's & All Saints, Glanmire, is famous for its elegant tower and spire. It was initially erected in 1784, on a site given by R. Rogers. One of its most famous patrons was Sarah Curran (1782–1808). Born in Newmarket, County Cork, she was the daughter of the prominent lawyer John Philpot Curran. While living in Dublin, Sarah fell in love with the United Irishman Robert Emmet, who was executed in 1803. Disowned by her father, Sarah uprooted to Cork, where in 1805 she married Captain Henry Sturgeon in the Glanmire Church. St Michael's Church in Upper Glanmire was dedicated and reopened for worship in 1808 following major restructuring.

Dunkettle House: At one time the vicinity was enlivened by many plantations, hanging woods, and a number of gentlemen's seats and villas. Built *c.*1790, Dunkettle House is a detached nine-bay, two-storey elegant Georgian country house retaining features exhibiting fine craftsmanship and materials. It was the family home of Abraham Morris, a wealthy Cork merchant and MP.

Almshouses: The three early nineteenth-century almshouses retain much of their historic and architectural character. They were built for the purpose by the Colthurst family of Blarney Castle. The family supported many nineteenth-century Cork charitable institutions, and also held several and important tracts of land to the north and north-east of Cork City.

Tudor-style arch: Built *c.*1810, this freestanding and former stone entrance gateway to Glen Mervyn House is an eye-catching landmark in the village. The Buildings of Ireland project denotes the 'decorative qualities of the Gothic style of the nineteenth century, using motifs from medieval domestic building in largely classical forms'. The current house was built *c.*1870 and possibly incorporated fabric from an earlier house.

Community Centre: The Riverstown community centre is a detached thirteen-bay, one- and two-storey former school, dated 1835. Cut stone is evidence of skilled nineteenth-century craftsmanship of stonecutters and stonemasons.

St Joseph's Church: The beautiful Roman Catholic St Joseph's Church in Springhill has a prominent position and is highly visible from the main road. It was dedicated in 1837. Its possible architect is Michael Augustine O'Riordan. The John Hogan sculpture is a significant interior feature as are features such as timber-panelled porch doors and confessionals, the carved timber gallery supported by fluted Ionic columns, and the carved marble altar furniture.

Vienna Woods: Built in 1903, the house was built to replace an earlier house destroyed by fire. The Buildings of Ireland project relates that that the construction and craftsmanship are of a very high quality and 'displayed in the cast-iron veranda supports, timber sash windows and cut limestone details'. Large additions to the original house were built in connection with its use as a hotel (after 1950). The historic character of the building can still be viewed.

A satellite quarter: With a current population of 15,498, Glanmire is used generally by residents of the area to refer to the Greater Glanmire area, encompassing Riverstown, Brooklodge and Sallybrook areas.

The Caverns of Carrigtwohill

The placename Carrigtwohill has been spelt several ways over the centuries – previous versions include Karrectochell (1234), Carigtothel (1285), Carrugtochil (1291), Carrectothell (1338), Carrigtoghill (1500s) and Carrigtoughill (Down Survey 1654–59). Local folklore and the work of local historian Liam O'Buachalla suggest Carraig Tuathghaill could connect to a personal name. He suggests it is probably that of a local landowner or petty chieftain. He also proposes that another explanation is *Tuathail*, which means awkward or out of the ordinary. Untypically for the district, the underlining rock strata has a northern aspect.

Subterranean layers: An outcrop of limestone rock to the north-east of Carrigtwohill is honeycombed with caves; some are very extensive, extending for miles underground, where beautiful stalactites are to be found. In the townland of Terry's Land a limestone cave system was explored by John Coleman during the 1930s and '40s. A wolf skull and domestic fauna were recovered.

Stone Age lithic scatter: In the townland of Clyduff, just east of Carrigtwohill, a find of flint arrowheads and waste was made by a landowner during ploughing. These are rare to unearth and provide important insights into the prehistory of the region.

Claidh Dubh: According to local historian Tom Barry, the western confines of Clyduff townland forms part of the Cliadh Dubh, a linear earthwork. It dates prior to AD 100 and has three sections, the longest of which runs north–south for 24km from the Ballyhoura Hills to the Nagle Mountains, passing over the Blackwater River. The feature is celebrated on Fáilte Ireland's Ancient East trail. The ditches take their names from Gaelic folklore. Their purpose and function are unclear. Regional folklore tells of several possible functions, from being some sort of territorial boundary to being an ancient trail, to acting as defence of cattle from wild animals.

Ruinous Parish Church: On the northern side of Carrigtwohill village is a rectangular graveyard enclosed by a stone wall. In the centre, the partially roofed remains of a late medieval parish church and its tower dominate. During this time, the village was part of the common of Barryscourt Castle. By 1615, the nave was in repair but the chancel was ruinous. The nave was maintained as Church of Ireland until the new church was built in the north-west corner of the graveyard in 1905.

Fattening Horses: In 1750, the historian, Charles Smith described Carrigtwohill as 'a small village seated on an arm of the sea which at high water flows under a bridge and overspreads a large tract of land making an excellent marsh for fattening horses'.

Fair Town: By 1795, Carrigtwohill had developed into a fair town, comprising over 100 houses. A ferry moved between Barryscourt and the opposite shore of Great Island until the start of the nineteenth century.

Saint Mary's Roman Catholic Church: The foundation stone of the present Catholic church, St Mary's, was laid on 4 November 1869. The architect was George Coppinger Ashlin and the church was built from local sandstone by Newstead Builders of Fermoy, at a cost of £2,500. The design mirrors another later and local work created by Ashlin: that of the Glounthaune Sacred Heart Roman Catholic church (1896).

Gaelic League: Local historian Tom Barry writes that an early branch of the Land League in County Cork was formed in Carrigtwohill in 1879. One of the key founders was the curate Fr R.M. Lynch, who also played role in the establishment of the GAA club.

The Land League sought fair rent, free sale and tenure. On their refusal to pay rent, many families in the Carrigtwohill townlands of Carrigane and Ballintubber East were evicted. Landlords were boycotted and police was posted in Ballintubber in a field still known locally as the Barrack Field.

Saint David's Church: In 1905, the Church of Ireland community finished the construction of a new Saint David's Church, financed by Lord Barrymore. This bordered an old structure, which had been in use since 1676. In 1995, the church was reordered as a community space – that of St David's Centre.

National Ploughing Championships: In 1992, the *Cork Examiner* recorded that approximately 140,000 people attended the National Ploughing Championships at Ballyadam in 1992. Another highly regarded national event, the Irish Open, was staged at Fota, one of the parish's two golf courses, in 2001 and 2002.

Satellite town: This village is now one of Cork's satellite towns, with modern housing estates where a population of 6,665 individuals live (2011). In recent years it has seen a 64 per cent increase in population, which has earned it the title of the fastest-growing town in Munster and the fourth fastest-growing town nationally.

The Manor of Midleton

The foundation by the Barrys or Fitzgerald Anglo–Norman families of a Cistercian monastery called Chore Abbey in 1182 gave Midleton its original and ancient name – Manistir na Corann. The abbey is still commemorated in the Irish name of the town. It was located on the banks of the Owencurra River and was dissolved in 1543, and the site was granted to a succession of new landlords.

The Middle Town: The present town derived its English name from its situation at equal distances on the road from Cork to Youghal ('the middle town'). Although the town was granted to Sir John Broderick, an English officer, in 1653, the name Corabbey was retained until 1670. In that year, the town received its charter of incorporation from Charles II. The Broderick estate constituted the manor of Midleton; both his castle and lands were made a free borough and he was granted a corporation of councillors to operate the manor and growing settlement within.

Remains of the Abbey: Set back on western side of Main Street in Midleton is an L-shaped graveyard, which is supposed to mark the site of the Cistercian abbey of Chore. The remains of the abbey were taken down to afford a site for the present church, St John the Baptist Church of Ireland (est. 1825). St John's is located to the south of the centre of the graveyard. No upstanding remains of the abbey remain but some stones from it lie in the graveyard and include a latern medieval door head and a piece of circular shafting.

The graveyard has a large collection of eighteenth- and nineteenth-century headstones and table and chest tombs. The earliest noted headstone is dated 1698. It is a rectangular slab, decorated at the base only with an angelic form with trumpet, surmounting a skull-and-crossbones, symbolic of resurrection and mortality.

A Market Town: By 1685, Midleton was noted for its broad main street. This was laid out not simply as a thoroughfare linking Cork to Youghal but as a market place. The street already contained a fine

Main Street, Midleton, *c*.1900 (source: Cork City Museum)

market house, the first civic building in Midleton, which acted as the town hall and housed the shambles, or meat market. By 1750, the market house had a public clock. The present market house, housing the library, was reconstructed in 1789.

The seventeenth-century college: Midleton College was established in 1696 by Elizabeth Villiers, a favourite of King William of Orange. It was housed in a newly constructed handsome limestone building, which is still in use today. It took in its first pupils in 1717. Some famous pupils comprise John Philpott Curran, (lawyer and father of the famous Sarah Curran), Edward Hincks (orientalist), Isaac Butt (founder of the Irish Home Rule Party), Standish O'Grady (literary pioneer), Rev W. Spottiswood Green (mountain explorer), and Rachael Kohler (international hockey player).

The Coppinger Granary: By the middle of the eighteenth century, Midleton had a reputation as a good market for 'flesh and fish'. Its produce attracted the attention of industrialists. The Coppingers of Barryscourt sought a site for a granary for the export of grain in 1791. By 1794, they needed a site for their brewery, which was built at the southern end of the Main Street. The nearby port of Ballinacurra was developed at this time to export grain to Cork and further afield.

Industry Cometh: In 1796, Marcus Lynch established the first factory in Midleton, next door to the Coppinger's brewery. Lynch hoped to employ 1,200 men and women and children producing woollen products, but the economic difficulties caused by the Napoleonic Wars forced him to close the factory in 1803 and sell it to the government for use as a barracks. In response to the new excise laws, the Hackett brothers of Cork had established the first commercial distillery on the Mill Road in 1824. The Murphy Brothers, also from Cork, bought Marcus Lynch's disused woollens factory and established their distillery. The profits from their distillery allowed the Murphys to establish the Lady's Well brewery in Blackpool, Cork, a few years later.

Midleton Distillery: From 1825 until 1975, the Cork Distilleries Company operated in the same buildings just off the main street. When a new distillery was opened, the old distillery was beautifully preserved and is now one of the most striking and interesting tourist attractions in Ireland. Taking the tour, the visitor can experience some of the original buildings, which date back to 1795, when they were just part of a mill complex. (before being converted for use as a distillery). The water wheel, which once operated all the machinery at the distillery, still turns and operates the cogs and wheels in the mill building today.

Advent of the Presentation Order: The Presentation Sisters arrived at Midleton in 1834. The convent was built on a site granted by Lord Midleton and financed by the Coppinger Family and Gould Trust Fund (which had been set up in 1826 for the promotion of Catholic education in the Diocese of Cloyne).

   The adjacent primary school was opened in 1834 and St Mary's High School was opened in 1902. In recent years, the old buildings have been demolished and replaced by contemporary convent accommodation. The ornate oratory and the graveyard for the sisters is now a quiet space of reflection.

Further additions: The present St John the Baptist's Church was completed in 1823 and the courthouse was built in 1829, both designed by the Pain Brothers. Unusually, Midleton's population increased during the Irish Great Famine as it had the only workhouse in East Cork until the Youghal workhouse was completed in 1849. The Midleton workhouse is now the site of the local hospital.

Railroad project: On 6 January 1845, a public meeting assembled in Midleton Courthouse to press for the building of a railway to link the three East Cork towns of Queenstown, Midleton and Youghal, with Cork and Waterford. The railway was completed between 1858 and 1862, but without the link to Waterford. The line ran until 1988. In recent years the line to Midleton has been reopened (30 July 2009), and is one of the busiest commuter lines serving Cork, carrying almost half a million passengers every year.

Holy Rosary Church: The Holy Rosary Church was dedicated in 1896. It was completed close to the site where Bishop William Coppinger had aspired to build a cathedral for the Diocese of Clyne in 1805. The church was designed by George Coppinger Ashlin, a leading church architect of the Gothic style and one of the designers of the Cobh cathedral. On 28 June 1908, the spire, tower and belfry were completed and blessed. It took eighteen months to be constructed by local builder and contractor Mr J.J. Coffey. The spire rises to 189ft and the beautiful copper cross, which surmounts it, is 12ft in height. The masonry in 1908 was noted by the *Cork Examiner* as 'bold, pitch-faced ashlar, butresses being finished by neatly wrought iron weatherings'. The bell is one of the largest in County Cork and was cast by Mathew O'Byrne, of Dublin. George Coppinger Ashlin also built the extravagant Munster and Leinster Bank opposite Midleton courthouse in 1900. This now houses the Allied Irish Bank.

War of Independence Monument: The Clonmult War of Independence memorial was designed by Seamus Murphy in 1932. The memorial commemorates events on 21 February 1921 when Irish Republican Army volunteers occupied a farmhouse in Clonmult, Co Cork. They were encircled by members of the British Army, Royal Irish Constabulary and Auxiliaries. Twelve IRA volunteers were killed, four wounded and four captured. A total of twenty-two people died in the ambush and the executions that followed. Fourteen IRA members, two Black and Tans and six suspected informers lost their lives.

A Village of Sculptures: For decades the Clonmult Monument was the principal one on Midleton's Main Street. In 1998, a second monument was added just a couple of metres away. Then in the early 2000s came the Gyrator on the site of the former Goose's Acre, again, not far from the original Monument.

In their 2013 budget, Midleton Town Council approved a number of capital projects for the period 2013–15. Five new sculptures, with the help of an open competition for entries, were commissioned to help the promotion of history, heritage and tourism in the town. Four of them were to be located in the area around the Clonmult Monument and one isolated in the park on the Bailick Road. Both 'Geese Attacking Young Boy', and the sculpted piece of Nellie Cashman are located at the Goose's Acre. 'The Fenian Man' is to represent the Irish 1798 rebellion by the United Irishmen movement. 'The Fair Green' is a concrete pillar finished with a granite face 3m high and has five oversized sheep situated around it. The fifth sculpture represents a Native American Choctaw gift of aid to Ireland during the Irish Great Famine. It is a bowl structure made of eagle wings 5–6in height entitled 'Kindred Spirits'.

The Banks of Ballinacurra

In 1824, a new line of road was opened, forming a western entrance to the small village of Ballincurra. Its location adjacent on a creek leading into Cork Harbour meant it possessed all the advantages of a small seaport, which the town of Midleton could access. In Samuel Lewis's *Topographical Dictionary of Ireland* (1837) Ballincurra is described as having one main street, from the centre of which another branches off to the east. Samuel Lewis further writes that the village

Ballinacurra, Midleton, *c.*1900 (source: Cork City Museum)

contained approximately 250 houses, most of which were uniform in design. The inhabitants were supplied with water from springs:

> There are two rivers: the Avannachora, or Midleton River, which flows on the west of the town and falls into the inlet about a mile below it, and the Rocksborough River, which skirts the southern part of the town and flows into the former river. Both rivers at one time were well fished and abundant with salmon and trout; over each river existed stone bridges.

A Creek of Quays: In the mid-nineteenth century the quays were accessible to vessels of 300 tons which could unload their goods safely. There were also some large storehouses, where coal, timber, iron, slate, and other heavy goods were landed and warehoused. These are now apartment complexes for modern-day living.

Export Port: Samuel Lewis in 1837 records that Ballinacurra warehouses were large spacious stores for grain, large quantities of wheat and oats which were annually shipped to Liverpool and Bristol markets. A deputy water-bailiff was stationed in Ballinacurra to collect the dues claimed by the Cork Harbour Board and the foundling hospital of the city.

Malt to Holland: In 1961, malt made entirely from barley grown in East Cork and manufactured at the maltings of Messrs J.H. Bennett and Co. Ltd Ballinacurra, on behalf of Irish Malt Export Ltd, was exported to

Holland. The malt was for use by a firm of Dutch brewers. This is the first time that malt had been shipped from Ballinacurra to Holland.

Closure: The port of Ballinacurra closed in 1962 as it was believed too costly to dredge the increasing levels of silt and mud at the entrance to the small harbour. It is now utilised almost entirely by small leisure boats.

The Cove of Cobh

In the late eighteenth century, Cobh was a small village named Cove. Built across the townland of Kilgarvan where an ancient church is reputed to have stood, the settlement just comprised a few scattered houses inhabited by families involved in fishing and boats. Through investment in its infrastructure by the local gentry family of Lord Midleton, the village grew into a town, which provided a central focus for accommodating shipping in Cork harbour. The extent of such shipping is recorded by pilots during the early nineteenth century, who noted that the advent of the Napoleonic wars could bring 600 merchant vessels at anchor nearby in the harbour. Over 400 sailing ships are recorded leaving the harbour under convoy in a single day. After Queen Victoria first visited the town in 1849, the port of Cove was named Queenstown in her honour. After the Irish independence of 1922, the town was renamed Cóbh.

The Promenade Quay: In April 1804, the finance bequeathed within the will of Mr Smith Barry directed that a new quay be built at Cove. This

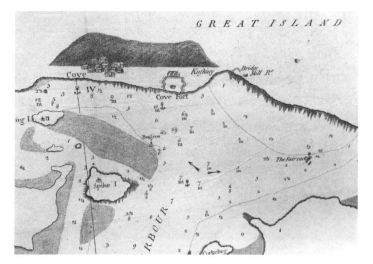

Map of Cove, 1788 (source: Cork City Library)

is now the Promenade Quay, which used to be called the Columbine Quay. The little pier at its west end was built by the Passage Railway Company for its steamers when they ran up to Passage.

Lord Midleton's interventions: In the early nineteenth century the Lords of Midleton were responsible for the development of the thriving town and commercial port. The courthouse and library was built in 1806 as a market house. St Mary's Protestant church and parts of the Midleton Road were also constructed about this time. Lord Midleton had quays and houses built along what is currently known as the East and West Beach. In the same year, Cobh again became a naval station and the Admiralty returned. Lord Midleton improved the road into the town, now known as High Road, the Esplanade and villa-type houses in Midleton Park. The fine crescent of thirteen houses, above Market House, was also built during this period.

Architectural treasure trove: Cobh is built into a hill, which has challenged architects through the ages to build the settlement on inclined streets. Walking Westbourne Place and West Beach alone reveals old quays and wharfs, historic townhouses and public houses, town halls and liner ticket halls. For example, check out west to east

Sketch of Cove by W. H. Bartlett, *c.*1841, from *The Scenery and Antiquities of Ireland* (source: Cork City Library)

railway station (1862, see Chapter 7, *Connecting a Harbour*), the former Royal Cork Yacht Club (1854, now the Sirius Arts Centre), Methodist Church façade (1873), Commodore Hotel (*c.*1855). the former White Star Line Office (*c.*1870, now Titanic Bar and Restaurant), Cobh Cabs Kiosk (*c.*1890), the fine Italinate structure and archway of the former town hall at Casement Square (*c.*1855), the former offices of the Cunard Line (*c.*1890, now Permanent TSB) and the elegant former Cork Harbour Commissioners Office complete with lighthouse-like tower (1874).

St Colman's Church

Medieval inspirations: Begun in 1867 and completed in 1919, decades of careful planning went into St Colman's Cathedral (named after the patron saint of the diocese). The great cathedrals of medieval France such as Chartres and Amiens inspired the architects to harness their designs. Designed by Edward W. Pugin and George Ashlin, it is one of the finest examples of ecclesiastical architecture in the Gothic revival style in Ireland.

Deep foundations: As the foundations were dug from steeply sloping rock, it was necessary in some parts to sink 24ft below the level of the future floor of the church, while in other parts a firm foundation was found at a depth of only 4ft. The preparatory work for the cathedral was difficult and expensive. The widening of the roadway on the seaward side required the construction of a high, long, and thick wall of solid masonry. The first sod of the foundations was turned on 25 April 1868 and the foundation stone was laid on 15 July 1868.

Four decades of construction: The church took forty-seven years to build – guided by three bishops. The first mass was held on 15 June 1879 with the official consecration day on 12 August 1919. A statue of St Colman stands over the west entrance. It was executed by Dublin sculptor Joseph O'Reilly. Created in 1890, it stands 8ft high and weighs 2½ tons.

Those who built it: The building contractors employed in the vast cathedral project comprised local quarrymen, car men, labourers, limestone and bath stone masons, sawyers, nailers, carpenters, smiths, plumbers, tradesmen's helpers and numerous general stone masons.

Design materials: Richly embellished and impressive in its design, the cathedral interior boasts different forms of stone and marble, which connects the cathedral to other Irish, European and American landscapes. Dalkey blue granite and Mallow limestone were used in the external walls. Fermoy red marble is used in nave columns, which rest on Italian white marble. Midleton red marble is used in shrines and in the first confessionals of both aisles. Connemara green marble is used in sanctuary pillars. Kilkenny black marble is used in engaged columns at the end of the north aisle. Italian white marble is used in communion rails and altar tables. Caen (Brittany) stone is used in stations of the cross. Californian pitchpine is used in the ceiling of the nave and in seating. Austrian oak is used in screens, the Bishop's throne, the canons' stalls and the pulpit.

Carillon: Cobh Cathedral Parish boasts a forty-nine-bell carillon belonging to St Colman's Cathedral. It is the largest in Ireland and Britain and also includes Ireland's largest bell, St Colman (3.6 tons). The carillon is played from a console in the belfry, comprising a keyboard and a pedalboard. The action is entirely mechanical and there is no artificial assist.

Queenstown Bridewell Prison: In 1992, an old prison was discovered after a 'sink hole' opened up beneath the cathedral car park and the main road outside St Colman's Cathedral. Local historian John O'Flynn has long campaigned for the old prison to be opened up and be incorporated as part of the tourist trail of Cobh town. In his research he discovered that the formerly-named Queenstown Bridewell Prison in Cobh was opened in 1845 and closed in 1985. The prison was primarily for men and women and tens of thousands were incarcerated there during its operational period. Between 1880 and 1895 records show more than 2,000 convict juveniles were also held there, many under the age of 12. In 2014 a memorial stone placed atop the closed-up site to commemorate its existence was co-funded by local church authorities and Cork County Council.

Wanderings in Whitegate

Ruinous graveyard: In the heart of Whitegate is an overgrown ruined church, with numerous headstones. The earliest headstones are noted as dating from the 1780s. Immediately outside the eastern end of the northern wall is a brick-vaulted mausoleum. It is reputedly the burial place of the local Roche family. This was the parish church of Corkbeg. It was in repair in 1615 but out of use by 1700. The new Church of Ireland church was built in the south-west corner of the graveyard in 1843. It is no longer evident, as it was replaced by a new church built on a site immediately south of the graveyard in 1881. St Michael's Church is still in use.

Queenstown 1860 by John Brandard (source: Cork City Library)

Queenstown *c*.1865 by Robert Lowe Stopford (source: Cork City Library)

Whitegate, 100 years ago: Guy's *Directory of Cork* for 1914 records Whitegate as a village with small well-built houses, where a considerable fishery was carried out. At one time several boats were employed as well in raising sand from the harbour, which was used for manure. The surrounding countryside was described as very fertile and is embellished by several elegant mansions, the principal of which was Corkbeg House, the residence of the Fitzgerald family. The house and part of the estate were built upon by Whitegate Oil Refinery. The refinery was officially opened on 22 September 1959. Its annual capacity was initially proposed to supply Ireland's total petroleum needs of 262 million gallons (see more in Chapter 9).

Memorials: A historic freestanding limestone fountain, erected in 1873, forms a focus in Whitegate. The level of craftsmanship involved in the construction is of the highest quality. The fountain serves as a reminder of the skill of local stone masons and sculptors available in Ireland at the time of its construction. It provides important context to the locality and forms an attractive roadside feature. Inscriptions read: 'A M D G July 1873 Erected by Robert U P Fitzgerald Esq For the use of the public. J Lynch Builder'. Nearby is a small green where today members of the Whitegate Petanque Boules Group meet and play. Adjacent lies a monument to those Aghada citizens who lost their lives in the First and Second World Wars.

Aspiring Aghada

Longforde: A house now exists on the site of Aghada Castle. The castle is shown on a 1587 map and named 'Longeforde'; 'Longeforde' is probably derived from 'longphort', a former Viking naval camp. The name survives at nearby Long Point.

Iron-smelting furnace: In 2003, an initial test excavation by the Archaeological Services Unit, University College Cork, at a proposed modern house site revealed the presence of a black charcoal-enriched feature. The site was on the main street in the village of Aghada between a two-storey dwelling to the south and a cottage to the north. The feature was then excavated. Archaeologist Annette Quinn, in her subsequently published report, writes about the high incidence of iron slag and tuyère fragments recovered from the main fill of the trench. She suggests that it was part of a furnace or a feature associated with iron working. The thick clay lining at the base of the trench is also characteristic of iron smelting furnaces. A shard of post-medieval pottery dating to between the seventeenth and nineteenth centuries was also found.

Ruinous graveyard: At the western end of Upper Aghada village is the roughly triangular graveyard with the ruined Church of Ireland parish church of Aghada. It is built on or near site of earlier parish church. At the base of the eastern window of the ruined church is part of an arch stone for a door surround of late medieval character. In 1710, an Act of Parliament granted permission to build 'a new parish church in a more convenient place'. In 1817, new church was built on a different site 300m to the north-west. The inscribed headstones date from 1711; one inscription is in Irish. There are numerous nineteenth- and twentieth-century headstones.

Presbyterian Church, Upper Aghada: Built in 1817, and formerly a Church of Ireland estate church, this building once formed part of a group of demesne-related structures. According to the Buildings of Ireland programme, its architectural style, in terms of its hall, tower and window openings, diverges from the typical early eighteenth-century Board of First Fruit-style churches. This is explained by its private patronage. It passed into the hands of a Presbyterian congregation in 1925, which is now the most southerly Presbyterian congregation active in Ireland. The interior retains characteristics of its Church of Ireland period, including its memorial plaques and the carved timber balcony.

Aghada, 100 years ago: Lower Aghada village is described in Guy's *Directory of Cork* 1914 as a seaside village. The small pier was originally constructed by subscription, where a steamboat from Cork or Queenstown called every Tuesday during the summer, and where coal and sand were occasionally landed. In the mid-nineteenth century about fifty local females were employed in platting Tuscan straw for exportation, and a few in platting the crested dog's tail, or traneen grass. Records from 100 years ago reveal that the parish of Aghada comprised 2,331 statute acres, as plotted under the Tithe Act: the greater part was under tillage, and nearly the whole of the remainder was pasture.

A new pier: On 2 July 1973, after 140 years, history repeated itself with the opening of the new pier at Lower Aghada. For the Lower Aghada Development Association it was the reward for years of endeavour. The pier was officially opened by Mr J.H. Foley, chairman of the committee. It replaced the old structure built in 1830. The old pier catered for the steamers *Audrey* and *Mabel*, known locally as the Greenboats, as well as the small cargo vessels, which were used to convey sand and other commodities to the quays in Cork City.

Saint Erasmus Roman Catholic Church: Dated to 1987, it is built on the site of an earlier church; the grave markers, earlier tower and foundation stone all add to its original story. The remains of a tower of an earlier church can be viewed just to the south of the present structure.

5

HOUSES, GENTRY
AND ESTATES

Corkbeg House

The fifty-roomed Corkbeg House was one of the best-known landmarks in Cork Harbour. The 150-year-old mansion was demolished in 1957 to make way for storage tanks for the Whitegate Oil Refinery. The history of the house was attached to the Fitzgerald family, beginning with the famous John Fitzthomas Fitzgerald, Lord of Connellan, Decies and Desmond. The Earls of Desmond were one of the most powerful families in Munster; several were Lords Deputy of Ireland in the fourteenth and fifteenth centuries. Gerald Fitzgerald, the sixteenth earl, resisted the Reformation in the reign of Elizabeth I and waged war against the English government.

After many battles, the Earl of Desmond's forces were defeated. On 11 November 1583 the Earl was killed in a glen near Castle Island, in County Kerry. His head was cut off and sent to England by Thomas Butler, Earl of Ormond. It was a present to Queen Elizabeth, who placed it upon London Bridge as a warning to others thinking of offering resistance to the crown.

Members of the Fitzgerald family retained their lands due to tenancy deals struck with the monarchy and local lords such as Boyle. In time, these lands passed down through the Fitzgerald family and Corkbeg House, the elegant residence of R.U. Penrose Fitzgerald, was constructed. The lawn and shrubbery were connected by a narrow slip with the main land, where the remainder of the demesne was situated, comprising 350 acres of some of the best cultivated land in the barony.

Fota House

Tours are given daily at Fota House, recounting the rise and fall of this stately mansion. The guides remind visitors that this was formerly an eighteenth-century hunting lodge, the centre focus of an estate on the

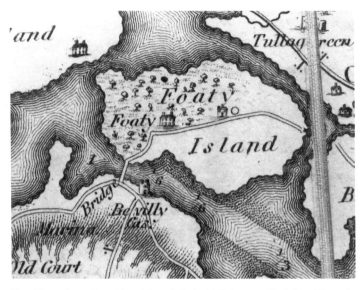

Fota House from Grand Jury Map of Cork, 1811 (source: Cork City Library)

780-acre Fota Island. In the nineteenth century the house was enlarged for John Smith Barry by Richard and William Morrison, architects for some of Ireland's finest buildings. The style of Fota House is classical throughout; the decor in the principal rooms reflects continental trends in the gilt, marble work, painted ceilings and magnificent plaster details.

John Smith Barry also embarked on a programme of works to turn the entire island into an estate of parkland, woods and pleasure grounds. The arboretum, with its beautiful orangery, formal walled gardens and 12 acres of parkland, was commenced in the mid-nineteenth century. Today the parkland boasts one of the finest collections of rare trees and shrubs grown outdoors in Ireland and Britain that is open to the public alongside Fota Wildlife Park and Fota Golf Course.

Fota Trust: The house began to deteriorate after the death of Dorothy Bell in 1975. She was the last of the ancestral owners to have lived in the house. After her death, it was bought by University College Cork (UCC) with former MEP Professor Raftery at the helm of the project that was to eventually become the Fota Trust.

Conservation assured: When the property was bought by UCC, its restoration was in the hands of Richard Wood and the conservation architect John O'Connell. Later work was supervised by the architect John Cahill, of the OPW, working with Dúchas Ireland's national heritage body and specialist groups from both Ireland and Great Britain.

Decorative detail: There are seventy-six rooms at Fota, all of which have a wealth of architectural and decorative detail. They reveal the craftsmanship and artistry employed both by the original builders and by the restorers who succeeded them. From kitchens to grand reception rooms, individual artisans throughout the ages of the house have left their signature behind.

Fota Tower: From the Cork–Midleton dual carriage way you get to appreciate local farmers' attempts at reclamation through the ages, and the broad mudflats, which serve as migratory birds' habitats. There are sections of the harbour to be viewed from the road, which seem almost forgotten. The Smith Barry tower house folly belonged to Fota House estate and exists on the edge of the Fota golf course. In the early nineteenth century, Smith Barry had the tower designed by Cork architect John Hargrave. It was built in a Tudor Gothic Revival style and its footprint can be seen from different locations surrounding it. It was used by the Smith Barry family as a hunting lodge. During the last part of the twentieth century the estate fell into disrepair. Fota House was restored but the folly was left to fall into ruin. The tower is homage to an interest in ancient history and stands tall as if reaching into its skyline, leaving its overall stone-blocked vision hanging poetically in the air.

Fota Wildlife Park: Opened in 1983, the 100-acre park is home to nearly thirty mammal and fifty bird species. It has made considerable investment in the past five years, upgrading its infrastructure, and is currently near completion of an additional 27 acre development that focuses on Asian animals and plants. In its promotional literature, it highlights that it is an independently funded, not-for-profit charity that is also one of the leading tourism, wildlife and conservation attractions in Ireland. The park has an average annual attendance of upwards of 440,000 visitors, making it a key tourist attraction in the southern region.

Lakelands, Mahon Peninsula

In 2003, preparation works for Mahon Point Shopping Centre complex revealed several features from the Lakelands estate: two access roads, a quay, and a number of garden features such as its icehouse,

Silhouette at Lakelands House, Mahon, of William Crawford, Junior (seated), by Edourt, nineteenth century (source: Cork City Library)

cellar and walled gardens. In the mid-nineteenth century, Lakelands House, the home of the Crawford Family was at one time the largest of almost fifty mansions in the Douglas Estuary region. By 1792, William Crawford had migrated from County Down to Cork, where he co-founded the successful Beamish and Crawford brewery. His son, William Crawford (Junior), continued his involvement with the brewery, but was also active in the cultural life of Cork City. He was one of the founders of the Crawford School of Art, of which his son William Horatio was a generous benefactor. From the 1890s to the 1940s, Lakelands was allowed to decay and is now occupied by a regional road and apartment complex, whilst the core of the former estate is marked by Mahon Shopping Centre.

Myrtleville House

Myrtleville is a small seaside village near Crosshaven. Frequented by Cork people and families through the ages, it had an important coastguard station protecting this section of the Cork coast. Today many holiday homes dot the local landscape. Nearby are the famous Fennell's bay and the other popular beach of Fountainstown. The shipping and merchant family of Trants owned Myrtleville House (still there) and farm. They built a cottage for family members, Myrtleville Cottage, which is now the well-known Bunnyconnellan Bar and Restaurant.

Rostellan House

The original Rostellan Castle was probably erected in the thirteenth century and may have originally been a Fitzgerald foundation. The earliest extant reference in 1565 shows that Gerald Fitz James MacSleyney sold his manor of Rostellan to John Fitzedmond Fitzgerald. In 1604, James I granted the town, castle and lands of Rostellan to Sir John Fitzedmond Fittzgerald of Cloyne forever.

Rostellan House from Grand Jury Map of Cork, 1811 (source: Cork City Museum)

The castle passed from Sir John to his son Thomas and from him to his son James, who married Mary Burke, daughter of Theobald Burke, lord of Brittas Castle. James died at Rostellan in August 1635, leaving his widow Mary to face troubled times. She had possession of it in 1645, when it was captured by Murchadh O'Brien, Lord Inchiquin, who entertained his friends there.

Murchadh let go his hold of it, except for a brief period, when Lord Castlehaven captured it. In 1648, Murchadh got a grant of Rostellan and this was later confirmed to him by Charles II. So the Fitzgeralds went out and the O'Briens came in. In 1708, William O'Brien, Earl of Inchiquin, granted to him and his heirs to have Rostellan made into a corporation with liberty to hold a weekly market and two fairs yearly, to enclose 500 acres as a park and to construct a quay.

William was also given title to 150 acres of slobland. At the same time, he took a lease of Haulbowline Island and in 1720, with others of the landed gentry of the area, formed the Water Club, the first yacht club in Irish history. Doubtless, William continued to reside in the old castle, as did a successor of his – another William, Earl of Inchiquin – who got a renewed lease of Haulbowline in 1765.

The wall at the west end of Rostellan demesne and its round tower had the appearance of a battery and there were four brass cannons pointing into the harbour. One of the cannons was made in Amsterdam in 1646, while the others were dated 1786, which may well have been the date of the building of the mansion house on the site of the old castle, and which incorporated parts of it.

There was a large two-handed sword in Rostellan House, said to have belonged to Brian Boru, which came into the possession of a Colonel Verdon of Clontarf Castle, Dublin, and a controversial statue of Admiral Hawke, which was bought by a Mr Green of Youghal.

After Dr Wise's death Rostellan House and estate was purchased by Sir John Pope Hennessy for £17,000. The last resident there seems to have been C.J. Ehgledew, one-time MP, who died in 1934. The house was demolished in 1940 and by 1949 the Cork GAA had bought the lands. Several estate features survive – a walled garden, now forested, and the crenellated waterfront wall. The slab from the house, carved with the arms of William O'Brien (1694–1777), is now in Cork Public Museum. Three cut limestone and impressive milestones on a wall of the nearby causeway to the south of the site date to 1734.

Trabolgan House

The shape of the bay gave Trabolgan its name – *Trá* meaning strand or beach, and *Bolgan* or *Bulgen* meaning 'bulging' or 'big wave'. Trabolgan House of the Roche family was once situated where the current swimming pool complex of the holiday centre is today. It was a Georgian house of two storeys at the front and three storeys at the back, the front of the house faced out to sea. Halfway up the current entrance avenue there is a triumphal arch similar in design to the Arc de Triomphe in Paris. A member of the Roche family is supposedly buried under the arch. The family coat of arms was removed from the house in the 1960s and now hangs over a house at Roche's Point.

In 1880, the Clarke family, of tobacco fame, purchased the house. Mr and Mrs Clarke resided at Trabolgan and even grew tobacco during the war years, until the late 1930s when Mr Clarke died and Mrs Clarke moved residence. The Irish Land Commission purchased the total estate from the Clarke family and most of the land (except some 140 acres) was divided amongst tenant farmers. The remaining estate including the house was used as a base by a unit of the Irish Army during the Second World War.

In 1947, the house was bought by a newly formed Cork Company, Irish Luxury Holidays Ltd, for a holiday camp to cater for about 300 guests. In 1958, Gaedhealachas Teo decided to buy Trabolgan house and estate and establish a boarding school for boys – Scoil na nÓg. This school was open from June 1959 and until 1973, and 160 pupils each year received their education through the Irish language. During the summer months, Scoil na nÓg operated a summer Irish college where up to 1,400 boys and girls were provided with an opportunity to improve their knowledge of the Irish language.

In the early 1970s, the site was bought by Dutch businessman Ernest Weeland, who sold it in 1975. BPF, a Dutch company representing the Dutch Metal Industry pension fund, bought Trabolgan and ran a small self-catering holiday homes complex in the estate until 1983. The planning of the new Trabolgan Holiday Centre wove into it the existing landscape elements of the seacoast, rolling meadow, woodlands, parkland, streams and lake, and enclosed and walled gardens. The central recreational area with pool, restaurant, bars, disco and bowling was built on the commanding site of the original Trabolgan House. An inscribed stone, which was found during demolition, read 'John Roche 1790'. Several estate features survive including the gate lodge, triumphal arch half way up the avenue, walled garden, Roche's Tower and a free-standing square chimney just to the north of the house, which according to local information was part of a gas works that provided light for the house.

The Dutch Metal Workers Union invested £20 million in Trabolgan and lost most of it, largely because the complex failed to attract significant numbers of English and continental visitors. It traded at a loss from day one.

Pontins bought the site for £5 million, promising a multi-million pound investment that included a 350-bed hotel and fifty new chalets. The hotel never materialised and neither did the thousands of extra visitors. In 1990, after changing hands a few times, Trabolgan was bought by Scottish & Newcastle Plc and has since undergone redevelopment programmes in 1991, 1998 and 1999.

Trabolgan House, early twentieth century (source: Cork City Museum)

6

PEOPLE, PLACE
AND CURIOSITIES

Huguenot and Hop Island

In the journal of the Cork Archaeological and Historical Society for 1909, an anonymous writer relates the story of Hop Island. Mr De La Main, a French Huguenot, arrived at Cork in the late seventeenth century. He possessed a small sum of money, the remains of a fortune, having left behind large estates in France. He pursued the career of dancing master for some time and was respected by the citizens of Cork. He purchased Little Island, built on it a beautiful residence and cultivated the adjacent grounds. The anonymous writer describes that the island was known previously as Ratland from the enormous swarms of Norway rats with which it was infested.

Due to De La Main's interest in dance, the sailors and boatmen used jokingly to call the island Hop Island, a name it has retained. Mr De La Main had a son Henry, an eminent composer of music, who was the organist of St Finbarre's Cathedral and Master of Ceremonies at the Cork Assembly Rooms. He was the author of a Book of Psalms set to music, which he dedicated to Queen Charlotte, which now maintains a high reputation as a masterpiece of sacred melody. Hop Island is now host to a popular equestrian centre.

Penal Laws and Mass Rocks

Due to the English Penal Laws of the eighteenth century, young men with Roman Catholic vocations for the priesthood had to seek education and ordination abroad. Many of them returned to Ireland to minister secretly, whilst others remained on the Continent, where not a few became illustrious churchmen. Over three decades ago, a plaque was placed on a rock on the East Ferry side of Great Island

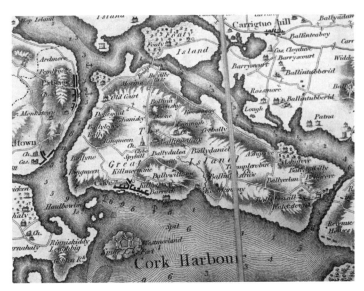

Great Island from Grand Jury Map of Cork, 1811 (source: Cork City Library)

where Mass was said on the shore during the Penal times. According to tradition, people used to congregate on the opposite side of the estuary to participate in the Mass.

In Templerobin graveyard in the village of Ballymore on Great Island lies the grave of Father John Shinnick. His grave stone carries a Latin inscription. Translated, it reads: 'Pray for me Here lies Rev. John Shinnick, who died on the 13th day of December in the 60th year of his age, the 27th year of his pastoral office, in the parish of the Great Island and in the year of Our Lord, 1721.' Being registered meant that he was the only priest permitted to celebrate Mass within an area prescribed for him. In 1704, Fr John Shinnick was registered in Cork as 'John Shinnick, residing in the Great Island, aged 40 years, parish priest of the Island and "Gurrane", ordained 14th Sept, 1694, at Antwerp, by the Bishop of Antwerp. Sureties John Hegarty of Great Island £50 and Darby Keeffe of Great Island, £50'.

A Pilgrimage of Heart, Our Lady's Well, Aghada
Located at Tileskin townland about 2 miles from Aghada on the farm of the Russell family, rounds are still performed every year at this holy well dedicated to the Virgin Mary. A remarkable stone stands by the well, which dates back to 1731, gives the pattern formula – seven

Paters, seven Aves and one Gloria. It is significant that the stone was inscribed in the year 1731 when nearly all the priests of Cloyne were on the run under penal laws.

On Sunday, 18 August 1878, John Windele, writer and antiquarian, visited Tileskin and there he saw the ruins of an ancient church and the pattern at the adjacent holy well. There were between 200 and 300 people there; 'all the blind, lame, and crippled men and women in the county, beggars innumerable, generally handsome young women with children in their arms'. The people were drinking the waters out of the well, which was handed to them in tumblers by a woman who stood within the enclosure. Over the well was a tree, on which they wore placing bits of rags—there were hundreds of bits. Near the well was a stone like a tombstone, around which were a number of blind men praying, and boys used to kiss the Christ-like figure cut on the stone in relief.

Cove 1787

From Richard Lucas's *Cork Directory* for 1787, printed by J. Cronin, 12 Grand Parade, Cork, it appears that at this time Cove possessed the following public officers: Henry Widenham, postmaster; Andrew Byrnes, quarantine surveyor; Wallis Colthurst [sic], William Dickson, and John Drury, tide surveyors, and George Mansfield, surveyor of excise. There seems to have been no lawyer there at this time; but there was a Navy surgeon, William Carr; L. Rancland, surgeon and man midwife; James Sall, surgeon and apothecary, and Patrick and Michael Fitzgerald, MDs. John Collins and Garret Barry were brewers, and James Simkins a vintner and brewer. William Barrett, John Clarke, of the Liverpool Arms, John Deace, James Donovan, and John Roche were boot and shoe makers. Philip Barry, Thomas Robinson, Robert Talbot, and John Verling were shipwrights; John Roche and Mary Cottam, ship chandlers; Michael Hartnett, silversmith; William Wilks, victualler; John Owlden, draper and Taylor [sic]; Edmond Bourke, Woollen and linen draper; William Martin, baker; Bartholomew Hide, tobacconist; William Gregory, tobacco manufacturer; Robert Carden, innkeeper; John Wood and Miss Mahony kept porter-rooms; whilst William King Sleigh was a tobacconist, grocer, painter and glazier. From this list it is evident that Cove could not boast of more than thirty places of business in the year 1787.

Edward Bransfield, Ballinacurra

Cork-born Edward Bransfield was born in 1785 to an important Catholic seafaring family in the port town of Ballinacurra, near Midleton. In 1803 when a British warship docked at Youghal harbour, the 18-year-old Edward joined the service of the Royal Navy. He had some maritime instruction from his father, who owned and traded his own boat.

Despite the onslaught of death during the Napoleonic Wars, he survived. Edward rose quickly through the naval ranks – first to the status of an officer and eventually achieving the rank of ship's master.

When the war ended in 1815, Edward Bransfield took up a post in the navy's new Pacific Squadron in Valparaiso, Chile. Whilst there, in 1819, a British merchant ship named the *Williams* made port recounting that it had viewed uncharted lands south of Cape Horn. Edward was sent to explore the account. He commandeered the Williams and led a crew of thirty men. They sailed 3,200km south from Valparaiso in December 1819. On 20 January 1820, Bransfield glimpsed 'two high mountains, covered in snow'. He had discovered what is now called the Trinity Peninsula, the northernmost point of the Antarctic continent.

What Edward Bransfield did not know is that three days earlier Russian sea captain Thaddeus von Bellingshausen had sighted 'ice mountains' near modern Queen Maud Land in Antarctica. Bellingshausen was never sure that what he had seen that day was land or just another iceberg. As for Edward Bransfield, he created detailed charts and documented the mountains and ridges he spotted. It was from this work that many scholars of the Antarctica credit Bransfield as the person who discovered the continent.

Today, in honour of his exploration work, Edward Bransfield is remembered through a number of named Antarctica landmarks: Bransfield Island, Bransfield Trough, Bransfield Rocks, Mount Bransfield and the Bransfield Strait. In 2000, Edward Bransfield was recognised for his discovery when the British Royal Mail issued a stamp in his honour. As no likeness of the man has survived, the stamp portrayed an image of the RRS *Bransfield*, a British Antarctic surveying vessel.

Memorials to Lord Hawke & Sarah Siddons

Lord Edward Hawke was a British admiral whose naval victory at Quiberon Bay, France, in 1759, put paid to French plans to invade Britain during the Seven Years War, 1756–63. It was believed Cork would have been the focus for a French attack, and, therefore, the admiral had saved Cork.

At the time, the citizens were exceedingly grateful and the corporation commissioned the artist Mr Van Nost to create a a statue of Lord Hawke, which was to be erected in the city. However, by the time the statue was finished in July 1766, Cork had lost interest in the heroic Lord Hawke — and refused to pay the artist.

The Inchiquins, owners of Rostellan Castle, with their long naval tradition, bought the statue. For many years, he stood happily on a plinth in the grounds of Rostellan Castle gazing over the harbour.

Near the Lord Hawke statue, on the boundary wall, stood and still stands the Sarah Siddons Tower, a place dedicated to the memory of the famous English actress, who played in Cork three times for the then enormous sum of 40 guineas a go. The Earl of Inchiquin greatly admired her and built a tower in her honour in his grounds. She, in turn, was apparently entranced by Rostellan and its scenery. Gradually, the monuments became weather-worn. Lord Hawke's right arm, which grasped a sword, reputedly fell off on the very day the French landed in Bantry Bay, in 1798. Eventually, the statue disappeared altogether and its whereabouts remains a mystery.

Old Church Graveyard, Cobh

The Old Church graveyard on Great Island reflects Cobh's history and its association with the world outside. In 1694, a Protestant church was built on the walls of the old church. It remained a place of Protestant worship until in 1815, when St Mary's Church was completed in the town (near Roches Row).

Within the ruins of a seventeenth-century church, which is in turn within the walls of this cemetery, are plaques to famous people who are buried here. The oldest grave is of Stephen Towse, a customs man in Cobh, who died in 1698. There are also tombs of the Scott family, to whom can be attributed the building of the square in Cobh and other buildings; they were ship owners and merchants and originally hailed from Bandon. The grave of Rev Charles Wolfe is inside the church walls. Charles Wolfe was made famous by his poem 'The Burial of Sir John Moore'. He also had many more poems published in *Barry's Songs of Ireland*. He died in Cove in 1823.

In the main graveyard is the Verling Tomb in which is buried Dr James Roche Verling, who was one of Napoleon's physicians after 1815. The remains of 169 victims of the sinking of the RMS *Lusitania* are interred here, mainly in three mass graves. Here also are crewmembers of the Royal Navy submarine *A5* who were killed in 1905 when a spark ignited petrol when moored at Queenstown. Six of the crew were either immediately killed by the explosion or died shortly afterwards.

The Republican plot is marked by a fine Celtic cross in which lie the remains of Captain James Ahern and Volunteer James Glavin, who were killed in action with ten of their comrades at Clonmult on 20 February 1921. Buried in the plot also are the men's two local comrades, Volunteers Maurice Moore and Paddy O'Sullivan, who were captured on that day and were later executed by firing squad.

Napoleon's MD, James Verling

Born in Cove in 1787, James Verling is best known for being Napoleon's medical adviser in his last years. In 1809 James graduated from Edinburgh University at the age of 23. He received a commission to be stationed at Ballincollig Military Barracks, Co. Cork. He later took posts with the Royal Artillery and was dispatched to the Peninsular War in Portugal.

When Dr Barry O'Meara Cork, Napoleon's first and favourite medical adviser during his captivity on St Helena, was dismissed from his post by British Governor of the island, Hudson Lowe, in July 1818, fellow Corkman Dr James Roche Verling was appointed in his place. He remained on the island for fourteen months and continued as official medical adviser to Napoleon. Verling was never permitted to attend to his patient.

James Verling left St Helena on 25 April 1820 and served in Malta, the Ionian Islands and then in Nova Scotia. Promoted up the ranks, he became Inspector General in 1854. On retirement he returned to Cobh and resided in Bella Vista, where he died on 1 January 1858.

Artist, George Mounsey Wheatley Atkinson

George Mounsey Wheatley Atkinson, who lived from 1800 to 1884, was a noted local maritime artist. He was untrained as an artist but was a seaman, and his understanding of the complicated rigging of tall ships is apparent in all his works. A number of his paintings, as well as those of the Atkinson family, are on display at the Crawford Art Gallery, Cork City. According to the *Dictionary of Irish Painters* in 1913, George was born in Cobh of English parents and went to sea as a youth working as a ship's carpenter. He later became Government Surveyor of Shipping and Emigration at Queenstown and was known locally as Captain Atkinson. He first signed paintings in 1841 and exhibited maritime paintings at the Royal Hibernian Academy (RHA) from 1842, showing many views of the entrance to Cork Harbour, Cobh, river views, the River Lee and scenes of ships. His painting of the *Visit of Queen Victoria and Prince Albert to Queenstown in 1849* was lithographed and published by W. Scraggs of Cork, and his volume, *Sketches of Norway*, was lithographed by his son and published by Guy and Co. of Cork.

Artist, Robert Lowe Stopford

In *A Dictionary of Irish Artists* (1913), the life of Robert Lowe Stopford (1813–98) is recalled. Born in Dublin in 1813, from his earliest years he exhibited an aptitude for art, and after getting some private tuition he settled in Cork while still a young man. There he built up a considerable reputation as a painter of landscapes and marine subjects in watercolour. He was also a successful teacher. He painted many views of local parts, many of which were lithographed, such as *Queen's College, Cork, River of Cork, Cork Harbour, The Evening Gun*, and *Haulbowline Island*. A drawing of The Wreck of the Sirius in Ballycotton Bay in 1847 was lithographed by him and published in Cork. The *Dictionary of Irish Artists* also highlights that he exhibited at the Royal Hibernian Academy in Dublin between 1858 and 1884. A view from the drawing room window of Lismore Castle, exhibited in 1863, was selected as a £10 prize in the Art Union of Ireland. He was for many years an art correspondent in the south of Ireland for the *Illustrated London News* and other papers. He died on 2 February 1898, at his residence, 2 De Vesci Terrace, Monkstown, Co. Cork, at 85 years of age.

Blackrock: A Fisherman's Village

In August 1843, a report entitled *Physical and Moral Condition of the Working Classes in the Parish of St Michael Blackrock near Cork* was read by North Ludlow Beamish, President of the Cork Scientific and Literary Society, before the statistical section of the British Association of the Advancement of Science at Cork. The population of Blackrock and its immediate environs in April 1843 was 2,630, consisting of families living in 413 houses. Ninety families lived in one-roomed houses, 260 in two rooms and 207 in three or more rooms. The trades Beamish listed were varied: brick makers (numbering 56), cabinet makers (2), carpenters (15), coopers (3), farmers (53), fishermen (111), gardeners (32), gingle drivers (13, generally owners), lime burners (18), masons (14), male servants (79), shoemakers (14), slaters (12), smiths (9), tailors (10). Male children numbered 426. As for female, their total was 1,133 with 372 employed as servants in work in fields. Female children, aged and infirm numbered 453, whilst 305 were unemployed. Beamish noted that wages for tradesmen were on average 20s per week; labouring men received 5s 10d; women 3s and children 2s per week but many men worked for 5s a week. In time of harvest, good reapers could be got at the ordinary wages of 1s a day.

Fr Mathew Tower

By the end of 1839, the reputation of the Cork Temperance Society, the first such known effective society in Cork City, began to spread further into north Munster. Driven by Fr Mathew, publicly acclaimed as the 'Apostle of Temperance' by the end of 1840, it is recorded that 180,000 to 200,000 people nationwide had taken the pledge.

Fr Mathew Tower overlooking Glountane was built as a testimonial to commemorate the work of Father Mathew, and was completed at Mountpatrick by Mr William O'Connor, opening with due ceremony on 9 November 1846. O'Connor, who had met with the Tipperary-born Fr Mathew in London's Strand, felt he deserved to be honoured in his home country.

An article on the opening in the *Illustrated London News* in 1846 notes that the graceful towers, one about 80ft high and another 100ft

Fr Mathew Tower, 1846, from *Illustrated London News* (source: Cork City Library)

high, were created for sightseeing over Lough Mahon. The overall structure was designed by George Pain, the architect of Blackrock Castle. On 9 November, a great number of invited ladies and gentlemen assembled in Mr O'Connor's demesne, and were given a tour. The article outlined:

> The visitors were first conducted to the second apartment, or what might be called the dining-room. It is circular, about sixteen feet in diameter. The windows are in the Gothic style, the upper portions being filled with stained glass. The window frames and cases are of fluted oak, and the latter are surmounted with carved heads; over these is some splendidly executed stucco work, which is continued along the entire ceiling, and gives the apartment a classic air. In a niche between two of the windows stands, on a handsome rose wood pedestal, and covered with a glass shade, an exquisite marble bust of the Very Rev. T. Mathew, by John Hogan.

Naturalist, Cynthia Longfield (1896–1991)

Madame Dragonfly is the biography of an Anglo–Irish woman who, despite her lack of formal education, became a world authority on dragonflies. Jane Hayter-Hames, niece of Madam Dragonfly, otherwise known as Cynthia Longfield, had the good fortune to have access to the journals her aunt kept throughout her adventurous life.

Born in London in 1896, Cynthia Longfield was the youngest of three daughters of Mountifort Longfield of Castle Mary, Cloyne, Co. Cork. Her father had inherited a substantial estate in Cork, although his income from it due to legislative reforms and pressure from many tenants to sell was not nearly as significant as his father had enjoyed. In the mid-1920s Cloyne barracks was attacked and burned by volunteers of the 4th Battallion of the Irish Republican Army. In their campaign against the English presence in this country the IRA turned their attention to the Longfield seat, which they also razed later that same year. While the castle was at the time valued at £50,000, the Longfields spent £5,240 on the conversion of the stables into domestic quarters. In her early years, Cynthia spent her summers in County Cork and the rest of the year at her other home in London. An ardent naturalist, from her earliest years she kept 'wildlife' in her bedroom and pursued her interest in the fields around her Cloyne home.

In 1923, and in grand old privileged fashion, Cynthia with her mother Alice and ber sister Norah, went on a voyage to Egypt. This afforded her the opportunity to study monuments, people and wildlife in a romantic and exotic setting.

In the ensuing years Cynthia's travels would take her on many thrilling and educational expeditions. One of the most fascinating of these was the Darwinian-like voyage of the *St George*. This vessel, funded by a private company, Scientific Research Expeditions Ltd, went to the South Sea islands to collect and study all aspects of wildlife. Cynthia, who had never received any formal education, scientific or otherwise, was signed aboard as an amateur entomologist.

Naval Heroes, John and Cornelius Collins

Twins John and Cornelius Collins were born on Easter Sunday, 1851, at Frenchfurze, Carrigaline, the sons of Bartholomew and Kathleen Collins, and attended Kilmoney National School. Living in close proximity to what was then a busy and strategically important harbour probably inspired the twins to join the British Navy at Queenstown at the age of 14 in 1865. Due to their age, the period of service for which they enlisted was in reality over thirteen years, for their careers in the navy proper were to commence from their eighteenth birthday for a period of ten years. They reported for duty to HMS *Hastings* at Queenstown and shortly after that were transferred to HMS *Narcissus* to commence their training. At that time Queenstown was the British Navy's Atlantic Fleet headquarters, and there was a Naval School as well as dockyard at Haulbowline and a training ship at Ringaskiddy. The brothers were promoted to the rank of ordinary seaman in 1869.

In 1871, the Japanese Government requested the British to assist in the modernisation and training of its navy, which at that time comprised poorly equipped wooden ships with crews badly in need of instruction in a rapidly changing maritime scene (e.g. steam ships). The Collinses were selected as part of a team of thirty-four British Navy instructors under Lt Cdr A.L. Douglas who travelled to Japan in 1873. John specialised in teaching gunnery to a Japanese marine battalion, whilst Cornelius lectured in seamanship and nautical matters at the Naval College in Tokyo.

The brothers were promoted to petty officers in 1876 and completed their official ten-year term of duty with the British Navy three years later, after they returned to England and Ireland. The Collinses, however, were back in Japan in 1879, this time as instructors in their own right on contract to the Japanese Navy (as well as an Englishman J. Woodword) and oversaw the development of a modern fleet until 1888, a period that included a number of naval skirmishes with Japan's Far East neighbours.

The Japanese fully appreciated the work of the two Carrigaline men. They were conferred with the Order of the Ki Ri medals as well as 150 yen (about a year's salary) and on 8 August 1888 were decorated with the highest honour a non-national could achieve: the Imperial Japanese Order of the Rising Sun plus diplomas. These were presented by the Emperor himself, Mitsu Hito.

Piper's Funfair

In the heart of Crosshaven still lies Piper's Funfair, the site of much enjoyment of adults and children alike. George Piper and his wife first came to Cork in 1878 and set up a funfair in Cobh. They had only one horse-drawn caravan, the side of which opened to form a rings stall. Later, as they expanded, they moved to the Marina (later occupied by Ford) and bought a house in Summer Hill.

When George died, his son Bill carried on the business and in 1910 took over the Sammy Field Funfair in Crosshaven. Bill had five sons and three daughters.

As the family grew, so did the funfair, with every year bringing a new machine and a new stall. In 1918, they opened in Douglas. During the Second World War, the Pipers became quietly known for their ability to acquire unavailable commodities like tea and sugar and imported fruit, much of which they distributed free of charge to needy families in the parish. They were also very supportive of the local church and to the local community.

The older generation remember that there were the chairoplanes, the stalls, the choice of winning a prize of ten bob, the shooting gallery, the one-armed bandits, the flying boats, the bumpers, the waltzers, the punchball, toffee apples, chocolates, penny bars, oranges, ice cream, Woodbines and the Cork fizzy drink Tanora. Then there were the lights, the hum of machines and the music. There were also the characters like Scott McLaren, who ran the roulette and who was a surviving engineer of the *Titanic* sinking.

The Statues of Annie Moore

From 1848 to 1950, over 2.5 million departed from Cobh in Cork Harbour. One of the most famous emigrant stories is that of Cork girl Annie Moore, who lived in Rowland's lane in Shandon, Cork City. She was the first passenger to be processed through Ellis Island Immigration Centre when it officially opened on 1 January 1892. Annie was 17 years old and was travelling with her two younger brothers, Philip and Anthony.

Their ship SS *Nevada* left Queenstown on 20 December 1891, transporting 148 steerage passengers. Across the North Atlantic, the journey took twelve days. Soon after their processing at Ellis Island, the young Moores met their parents, who had already emigrated to New York City.

In recent years, professional genealogist Megan Smolenyak discovered that the real Annie never left New York and also found some other important details. Late in 1895, Annie went to St James Church and there married Joseph Augustus Schayer, a young German–

American who worked at the Fulton Fish Market. She had at least ten children before dying of heart failure at age 50 in 1924. Her grave in Calvary Cemetery in Queens is marked with a Celtic cross composed of limestone imported from Ireland. She spent her entire life in New York's Lower East Side.

Today, Annie Moore is remembered by two statues sculpted by Jeanne Rhynhart – one at Cobh Heritage Centre (formerly Queenstown), her port of departure, and the other at Ellis Island, her port of arrival.

Willie Cosgrove, The Giant of Gallipoli

A simple Celtic cross in Aghada Cemetery is the memorial to a Cork soldier who has gone down in history as the 'Giant of Gallipoli'. For Willie Cosgrove, a corporal with the lst Battalion of the Royal Munster Fusiliers, the baking heat and atrocious conditions of 1915 in Gallipoli, Turkey, must have been worlds away from the peaceful greenery of Aghada.

Cosgrove, who joined the Fusiliers in 1910, was with the first wave of troops that landed at Gallipoli and valiantly fought to retrieve a desperate battle position. Fighting their way, inch by inch, off the beaches and up the heights of Sedd-el-Bahr, dominated by Turkish trenches and machine-gun posts, it represented a hell similar to that raging on the Western Front.

Corporal Willie Cosgrove has gone down in folklore as one of the few Irish soldiers who won a Victoria Cross and lived to talk about it. On 26 April 1915, during the early wave of attacks on the Turkish positions near 'Beach V', he led his section against the enemy lines on the hills dominating Cape Hellas, Gallipoli. The Turks, under the supervision of German officers, had carefully laid barbed-wire traps and entanglements to protect their positions from any assault. Sir Ian Hamilton, in his commentary on the landings, stressed that the Turkish entanglements 'were made of a heavier metal and longer barbs than I have ever seen elsewhere'. As the Fusiliers struggled to cut their way through the wire, they found themselves suffering terrible losses when caught in a terrible Turkish crossfire. Rushing forward with his section, Corporal Cosgrove, then 27 years old, single-handedly cleared the barbed wire despite the furious fire from Turkish positions both above and beside him.

Cosgrove, towering at 6ft 5in, tore the wire positions clear for his men and then followed them in their successful bayonet charge on the Turkish trench. As the action drew to a close, he was struck by a bullet, which tore through his side and passed out his back, leaving razor splinter damage to his backbone and partially crippling him for life. For his action in clearing the wire, he was recommended for the Victoria Cross and, on 23 August in the same year was gazetted with the British Army's highest honour for bravery in the field. Cosgrove was moved back to Aghada and then to England where he died, in Millbank, London, on 14 July 1936.

Titanic photographer, Frank Browne

Frank Browne was a passenger on the White Star Line's *Titanic* when the enormous liner stopped at Queenstown (Cobh) on 11 April 1912 on her maiden voyage. The theological student received the two-day trip from Southampton to Queenstown as a gift from his uncle, who was the Roman Catholic Bishop of Cloyne. Browne, a keen photographer, enjoyed recording many images of the new ship. When an American couple offered to pay for his onward journey to New York, he sent a telegram to his Jesuit Superior in Dublin for permission to remain on board. The response was clear: 'get off that ship'. Fortunately, Browne obeyed and the *Titanic* sailed from Queenstown without him. The ship sank on 15 April, with the loss of over 1,500 lives. Frank Browne's *Titanic* photographs provide a remarkable glimpse into life on board a liner that became one of the most famous and tragic ships in history.

Boxer and Actor, Jack Doyle, the Gorgeous Gael

Cobh-born Jack Doyle (1913–78) enlisted in the forces of the Irish Guards based in Wales in 1929. He quickly shone at boxing and was known for his tall frame and strong hooks that gained him the British Army Championship. He subsequently achieved a historic record of twenty-eight straight victories, twenty-seven by knockout. His wins led him to boxing promoter Dan Sullivan. Jack turned professional and attained ten victories, all inside two rounds.

In 1933 Jack Doyle's tenor singing voice was heard by Dr Vincent O'Brien, teacher to Count John McCormack. Very soon after he was performing at the London Palladium and The Royal in Dublin.

In 1934 Jack emigrated to America and carried on a life of drink, gambling, and ladies. His wealth and good looks led him to starring roles in two movies, *McGlusky the Sea Rover* (1934) and *Navy Spy* (1937).

Jack returned to Ireland with his new girlfriend Movita Castaneda (having recently split from his wife Judith Allan), a member of the Mexican aristocracy and Hollywood starlet. They organised a celebrity wedding in Dublin's Westland Row Church. They performed on both sides of the Irish Sea, selling out music halls and opera houses. In 1939 his popular signature song 'South of the Border' was recorded with his then-wife Movita by Decca Records, which produced many records of Jack singing.

In front of 23,000 people in Dublin's Dalymount Park, Jack fought his last professional fight, against Chris Cole. The inebriated Jack went down in the first round. Movita migrated back to Hollywood, where she married Marlon Brando. Shortly afterwards, Jack found himself being jailed at Mountjoy Jail in Dublin for punching an Irish Garda detective. He moved to England and his alcoholism and bankruptcy led his fortune to be spent. He died at St Mary's Hospital in Paddington and was buried in his native Cobh in the Old Church Cemetery in 1978.

Explorer and Naturalist, Richard Hingston

Passage West-born Richard Hingston (1887–1966) was an eminent explorer and naturalist. Graduating from the National University of Ireland with first-class honours in 1910, he obtained a position in the Indian Medical Service. In 1913, he was seconded from military duty as naturalist to the Indo–Russian Pamir triangulation expedition. In 1914, he arrived on the war fronts in East Africa, France, Mesopotamia and the Northwest Frontier. He attained the Military Cross for his service.

In 1920, he published a book detailing his 1914 and 1916 travels in the Himalayan valley of Hazara, in what is now Pakistan, entitled *A Naturalist in Himalaya*. He was elected to the Royal Geographical Society on 22 June 1922. In 1924, he was appointed medical officer and naturalist to the Mount Everest Expedition. As a naturalist he collected 10,000 animal samples (insects for the largest part), and 500 plant specimens during the trek. From 1925 until 1927, he served as surgeon-naturalist to the Marine Survey of India on HIMS *Investigator*. He wrote a lot and much of his work appeared in scientific journals. Almost all the specimens he collected are housed at the Natural History Museum in London.

Hurler, Nicholas Christopher Ring

Cloyne-born Nicholas Christopher Ring (1920–79) played hurling with the famous Glen Rovers club from 1941 until 1967. He was a member of the Cork senior team from 1939 until 1963. Former players, commentators and fans regard him as one of the finest players in the story of hurling.

Christy's status as one of the all-time greats is self-evident. His record of sixty-four appearances in championship games has yet to be equalled, while his tally of thirty-three goals and 208 points in these games was a record score, which stood until the 1970s. Christy's haul of eight senior All-Ireland medals, all won on the field of play, was a record, which stood for over a decade. Christy also won a record eighteen Railway Cup medals with Munster. No other player in the history of the competition has gone into double figures.

Athlete, Sonia O'Sullivan

Sonia started her running career in Ballymore Running Club on Great Island. For almost a decade and a half in the 1990s and early 2000s she was one of the world's foremost female 5000m runners. Her greatest success was a gold medal in the 5000m at the 1995 World Athletics Championships. She won silver medals in the 5000m at the 2000 Olympic Games and in the 1500m at the 1993 World Championships. She also won three European Championship gold medals and two World Cross-Country Championship gold medals. A statue to her achievements was unveiled in Cobh on 20 September 2015.

7

CONNECTING
A HARBOUR

Throwing the Dart

The importance of Cork Harbour was revealed in Henry VII's charter, dated 1 August 1500. Henry VII ended the dynastic wars known as the Wars of the Roses, founded the Tudor dynasty and modernised England's government and legal system. The waters of a harbour such as Cork were an English highway to move goods, people and ideas around. For Cork, Henry confirmed all former charters, and further granted that the Mayor and citizens, and their successors, could enjoy their franchises within the city, the suburbs, and every part of the harbour. The charter reveals the extent of land to be the metropolitan area in a sense in Cork Harbour:

CEREMONY OF " THROWING THE DART" BY THE MAYOR OF CORK.

Throwing the Dart ceremony with Mayor and officials, mouth of Cork Harbour, 1855, from *Illustrated London News* (source: Cork City Library)

As far as the shore, point, or strand called Rewrawne, on the western part of the said port, and as far as to the shore point or strand of the sea, called Benowdran, on the eastern part of the same port, and as far as the castle of Carrigrohan, on the western side of the said City and in all towns, pills, creeks, burgs, and strands in and to which the sea ebbs and flows in length and breadth within the aforesaid two points, called Rewrawne and Benowdran [better known by their modern names of Cork Head and Poer Head].

In time, and arising out of the Mayor having jurisdiction over the harbour, the ancient ceremony of Throwing the Dart emerged. It is unknown when the ceremony began – maybe *c.*1610 – and a similar ceremony began in Limerick in 1609 and Waterford in 1626. The earliest written record of the custom of claiming the waters in Cork is to be found amongst the archives of the Corporation and transcribed in a very insightful book by Richard Caulfield, entitled the *Council Book of the Corporation of Cork*, published in 1876.

Roche's Point Lighthouse

Around AD 1640–50, the Roche family purchased the Fitzgerald estate (approximately 1,500 acres) from Edmund Fitzgerald of Ballymaloe and lived for many centuries at Trabolgan. Roche's Point, at the mouth of Cork Harbour, is named after this family. In post-medieval times, a tower existed on the estate called Roches Tower. In 1759, this tower was taken down.

A letter dated 28 August 1813 from Vice-Admiral Thornborough of Trent, Cork Harbour, was read to the Ballast Board on 2 September 1813. In this letter he pointed out the danger in which vessels were put when frequenting Cork Harbour for want of a lighthouse at the entrance. A small lighthouse was working by June 1817 but its tower was not conducive to a major harbour of refuge and port, and in 1835 it was replaced by the present larger tower.

The year 1864 coincided with further additions to the lighthouse. In September it was decided by the Ballast Office in Dublin that the lantern at Roche's Point lighthouse be changed to a red revolving light, showing its 'greatest brilliancy once in every minute'. It came into effect on 1 December 1864. On the evening of 1 October 1864, a fixed white light was exhibited from the base of the lighthouse (a second light to the red one). This light was to shine seaward, between the bearings of S W by W and S W ½ S, or between Robert's Head and a distance of half a mile to the eastward of Daunt's Rock. Mariners were cautioned when approaching Cork Harbour by night to keep to the eastward of the limitations of the white light, until they had passed Daunt's Rock.

Roches Point, early nineteenth century by H. Morgan (source: Cork City Library)

A fog bell was also erected, which was to be sounded eight times in a minute during thick or foggy weather.

On 1 September 1876 two further improvements were made. The red revolving light in the lantern of Roche's Point lighthouse was changed to an intermittent white light, showing bright for 16 seconds, and suddenly eclipsed for 5 seconds. This gave a brighter and more easily distinguishable light. The other improvement was the substitution of a larger fog bell hung from a belfry and sounded twice in a minute, for that which had hitherto hung at the basement of the lighthouse and was sounded eight times per minute. The previous bell was of very little practical use as it could not be heard until a ship had got within the headlands. The new bell, on the other hand, could be heard sooner, at a greater distance, and more distinctly.

In March 1888, new tenants were sought for the valuable plot of ground immediately adjacent the lighthouse complete with signal tower and four dwelling houses, to be held for a long term at the yearly rent of £30. The houses had been availed of by the late owner as a commanding position offering means of communication with passing vessels.

By the early twentieth century, Roche's Point had a fixed light 60ft above high water with a visibility of 13 miles. It also has a recurring light, 98ft above high water, which can be seen 15 miles away in clear weather.

By July 1970, Roche's Point Lighthouse was all electric, with a Mandley generator to take over in case of an Electricity Supply Board (ESB) power failure. Formerly, the light functioned by use of vaporised oil through a special-type regenerative burner. The power of the light was also increased to being white 46,000 candelas and red 9,000 candelas.

By 30 March 1995, the presence of somebody physically watching out for mariners disappeared forever, at 11 a.m. when the three lighthouse keepers left the facility for good. The workings of the equipment became automated and were to be monitored from a lighthouse depot in Dun Laoghaire, Dublin. As to the fog horn, the Commissioners for Irish Lighthouses decided that, with modern shipping equipped with GPS navigation systems, the fog horn had become costly to maintain or replace, so it was no longer required.

Daunt's Rock Lightship

Daunt's Rock is between 4 and 5 miles from Roche's Point and was named after a Captain Daunt whose British man-of-war ship hit the rocks and sank in the earlier part of the nineteenth century.

Up to 1865, it was beyond the limit assigned to the Harbour of Cork by the British Navy. It was not marked on the Admiralty Chart of Cork Harbour. In April 1864, following the smashing of the ship *City of Cork* upon the rock, the Board of Trade strongly urged the rock be removed as soon as possible. They proposed, until its removal was implemented, to protect it by a light-ship. Engineer Sir John Benson was requested to make an accurate survey of the rock.

By June 1865, a bell boat beacon was placed to mark the position of Daunt's Rock. It was shaped like a boat, and was surmounted by a triangular superstructure of angle iron and lattice work, which was coloured black, with the words 'Daunt's Rock' marked in white letters on it. The ball on the top of superstructure was 24ft above the sea, and the beacon was moored within 120 fathoms SSW of the rock and in 12 fathoms at low water spring tides.

In September 1874, the British Royal Engineers received instructions from the War Office to immediately commence experiments with a view to blowing up Daunt's Rock, although this did not take place.

In late October 1896, in a gale, the lightship foundered on jagged rocks to the east of the ship's position. In early November 1896, a search party conducted operations under the supervisor of Captain Gallway and Captain Flewery of Irish Lights. Two divers went down in search of the eight-man crew and to review the injuries sustained by the ship. The large steel main mast on which was fixed the cage containing the light (and all the appliances in connection therewith) had completely gone over the port side and sunk in deep water. The mast was carried away beneath the deck. On reaching the ship's deck, with the view of exploring her interior so as to ascertain if the bodies of the unfortunate crew were entombed, it was discovered that the two entrances to the cabin were completely blocked with floating pieces of timber and other debris, which rendered it impossible for the divers to force an entrance.

In 1936, during a winter gale, the Daunt's Rock ship dragged her anchors and drifted some 3 miles off course, and was in danger of being driven ashore. The Ballycotton lifeboat and the British destroyer *Tenedos* both went to her assistance and stood by her for over three days. The *Innisfallen* of the City of Cork Packet Company, which had left Cobh, heard of the lightship's plight and although it was over three-quarters of an hour's steaming on its journey, it immediately returned to render assistance.

In early March 1956, the Daunt's Rock ship *Gannet* replaced the ship *Albatross*. The *Gannet* was the first of a new type of all-electric lightship, which had served for about a year on the Kish Station, near Dublin.

In June 1974, the Irish Lights commissioners announced that they intended to withdraw the Daunt's Rock lightvessel outside Cork Harbour and replace it with a high focal plane flashing buoy painted black and white. When the lightvessel was taken away in August 1974, radio beacons were established on the Old Head of Kinsale and at Ballycotton. The withdrawal followed the general pattern of Irish Lights policy. In the 1970s, four lightships on the east coast of Ireland were replaced by flashing buoys.

Spit Bank Light

Located on a sandbank, the Spit Bank lighthouse retains its original form and character. It is a freestanding cast-iron lighthouse, built in 1853, on a circular plan with cast-iron railings to a walkway and two-stage domed lantern on a circular plan. When it was built it was completely innovative as it used patented screw piles to anchor it to the mud bank. Belfast Engineer Alexander Mitchell lived in Cobh to supervise the construction. He was blind from the age of 20 and died in 1868 near Belfast at 88 years of age, leaving behind a legacy of screw -pile lighthouses, piers and bridges all over the world.

A Telegraph System

The *Gentleman's Magazine* for 1830 records that a meeting had been held of the Harbour Commissioners of Cork, at which it was decided to establish telegraphs and a code of signals for the harbour. Writer Colonel Grove White in the *Journal of the Cork Historical and*

Archaeological Society for 1904 highlights the telegraph system in Cork Harbour that was adopted. It consisted of four flagstaffs – one of which was placed on Roche's Point, the second on the high ground above Ardmanagh House, Passage, the third on Blackrock Castle, and the fourth on the Steamship Company's office, Penrose Quay, Cork City. When a steamer came into sight from London, Liverpool, Dublin, or Bristol, the flag was run up at the lighthouse, an answering signal was flown from the field on Passage hill, it was responded to from Blackrock Castle, where it was viewed from Penrose Quay, and the house flag, a cross of St George on a white background, was raised above the office.

East Ferry

For many decades up to 1923, a manually operated ferry popularly described as a pontoon-type bridge made five or six trips daily across East Ferry – across the eastern channel off Great Island to the general Rostellan area. The old Irish name of the ferry was *Caladh Ratha*, or, the ferry of the rath (ringfort). The *rath*, or *lios*, was situated near the

East Ferry of Great Island, wooden river ferry with horse and cart on board, *c.*1900 (source: Cork City Museum)

ferry point on the Great Island. It transported passengers, carts and cattle from shore to shore.

The barge, or bridge, as it was sometimes called, consisted of two pontoons, or covered boats, placed parallel with each other, and about 6 or 8ft apart. On top of those pontoons was built a strong wooden platform, with high railings around. At each end of this platform was attached an additional section with hinges, which allowed it to be dropped down on the strand in such a way as to be almost level for horses and cars to get aboard. This barge was moved across the channel by means of a chain and windlass. The barge travelled at right angles to the current, the bows of the pontoons faced the current, allowing it to pass through freely. This was a favourite trip for American tourists to come from Cove by sidecar. Information regarding its end is conflicting. Some locals say it was wrecked in a westerly gale in 1923. Others say it was targeted and rendered inoperative during the Irish Civil War. Local boating still exists in the area and the licence for the ferry is renewed for heritage reasons every year. The impressive Holy Trinity Church, Saleen, occupies the eastern bank of the east Ferry Passage. The site was given by Richard Wallis Goold Adams of Jamesbrook, the foundation stone was laid in 1885 and the church was completed in two years. The architect was William Atkins and the builder was a Mr Devlin. The interior was influenced by the works of English architect William Burges, who was notably the architect and designer of St Finbarre's Cathedral in Cork.

The News of the World

It was advantageous to Cork pressmen to intercept steamers off Cork Harbour and obtain the latest news hours in advance of their English counterparts. *Cork Examiner* editor Thomas Crosbie scooped the London papers in this fashion on several occasions.

Since 1853, a telegraph cable between Ireland and the UK had been in place. Recognising the potential of Cork, the Magnetic Telegraph Co. began to use tenders based in Cork Harbour to intercept steamers off Roche's Point and telegraphed their media dispatches via Cork and the Irish cable to London. They could best the international media company Reuters by several hours. American news was of vital interest in commercial circles, as fortunes could be won or lost on the basis of events in the US, and Reuters could not afford to be upstaged in this situation.

Both Reuters and the Magnetic Telegraphic Co made the same decision in 1862–63; the farther west they could intercept the news, the sooner the dispatches could be forwarded to London by telegraph.

The Magnetic Telegraph Company determined on Cape Clear as its base whilst Reuters based itself in Crookhaven, both in West Cork.

The Telegraph Connection

Up to 1860, to receive the news brought by the American ships as they docked at Queenstown it was necessary that the dispatches should be forwarded by telegraph, a distance of nearly 800 miles, or about half the entire length of the cable, which for a short time stretched across the Atlantic. When a steamer called at Queenstown, its news had to be transmitted from Cork to Dublin, thence to Belfast, thence to Donaghadee, across the Channel to Portpatrick from there to Dumfries, then to Carlisle and Liverpool, and finally to London. This involved great delay, and numerous breaks in the communication, and mistakes constantly arose from the repeated transmissions. That, however, was by no means all the delay. The steamers called off Roche's Point and a steamer was required to convey the dispatches up the harbour to Queenstown, the time taken being an hour and a half. There was no telegraph from Roche's Point to Queenstown.

In early 1862, it was proposed to establish a new telegraphic line, which would place Queenstown not only in direct communication with the telegraphic station at the entrance to the harbour but also with the Old Head of Kinsale, from whence the Atlantic steamer might be sighted several hours earlier than was then the case. Lord Fermoy gave permission to lay a telegraphic wire over his property at Roche's Point. On 1 April 1862, a timber signal pole, 130ft in height, and rising 230ft above the level of the sea, was erected at the lighthouse.

The line was to be carried on to Queenstown and join a main line which would connect Cork to Queenstown with Waterford and Wexford, and thence run to Carnsore Point, projecting a considerable distance into the St George's Channel. At this point the line was to be submerged to St David's Head, on the Welsh coast, and be continued through Milford, Gloucester, and Bristol, direct to London, the whole line requiring about half the time previously needed to connect Queenstown and London.

The Community of Pilots

From the beginning of history pilots with a specific local knowledge were required to guide ships in harbours and narrow channels. Medieval law stipulated that, in the case of a ship and cargo being lost by the inefficiency of a pilot, the crew could behead the pilot.

In the past, the pilotage area covered much of the south coast, west as far as the Mizen Head, as pilots raced to board ships in a free-for-all, but this was regulated later by the Harbour Commissioners in the nineteenth century.

In 1875, when 2,280 overseas vessels entered the Port of Cork, sixty-four harbour pilots and two Ballinacurra pilots were employed. Prior to 1892, there were sixty-seven sea pilots within Cork, whose average weekly earnings were from 12 to 15 shillings, old currency. The pilots brought the transatlantic liners into the harbour, and in stormy weather occasionally they could not get off, and had to remain on the liner on her journey to New York.

On 18 January 1877, a boat left Queenstown at dawn, with seven men, to meet ships coming into the harbour and seek orders. They went out on an open boat and travelled several miles to the south of Roche's Point Light, so as be the first to reach any approaching vessels. At 9 a.m. they met the British barque *G.J. Jones*, which was under the command of Captain Evans. The water clerk, McCarthy, and an assistant, went aboard the barque. The boat was tied onto the ship and was towed behind it for a quarter of an hour. The worsening sea conditions forced them to cast off the boat and they had to use their oars. When the ship was a mile away they saw the men in the boat standing up on the thwarts. The captain, with the aid of his glasses, saw that the boat was full of water. The pilot said that it would be too dangerous to 'heave to so near the land'. Therefore, no assistance was given to the boat and after a few minutes she went over. The five men left aboard were drowned.

In time, the number of sea and river pilots was reduced to fifty, but pilot boats were still kept on station at Mizen Head, Galley Head, Old Head of Kinsale and Cork Harbour's Mouth. Today the number of pilots is smaller again, with all pilotage the responsibility of the Port of Cork. Pilotage is compulsory for all vessels in the area between Number 20 buoy in the Lower Harbour and the Quays of Cork. For vessels exceeding 130m in length, pilotage is compulsory 2.5 miles off Roche's Point.

The Passage Lifeboat

The *Gentleman's Magazine* for November 1825 records that Andrew Hennessy, of Passage West, created a unique life or safety boat from replicas submitted to the Lords of the Admiralty and Trinity Board in London. The boat was 36ft in length along its keel and able to save fifty or sixty persons from a wreck. The timbers, which were very slight, were of oak, tarred and parcelled with light strong canvas, over which there was a casing of thin whalebone. The covering or skin of the boat, instead of a plank, was a special type of canvas, of great strength and long-lasting quality, and waterproof. The materials of the canvas had been drenched with a chemical process in the loom, which conserved it from dampness. The boat was decked or covered with the same cloth.

The Fishing Boat Community

Apart from busy commercial and naval dockyards, the harbour also provided a maritime space for small fishing communities from salmon fishers working in small open boats to the large sailing trawlers. These sailed as far as Youghal to the east and beyond Kinsale to the west. In addition, there were shrimp boats from Loughbeg, a small fishing community at Ringaskiddy. Power and speed were managed by means of brailing lines on the mainsail.

Cork, Blackrock and Passage Railway

The first sod for the Cork, Blackrock and Passage Railway was cut by Lady Eliza Deane at a site adjacent to the Deane Family residence at Dundanion in Mahon in June 1847. The *Illustrated London News* depicted this scene on 26 June 1847. In May 1847, the low embankment, which was constructed to carry the railway over Monerea Marshes, was finished. In Blackrock, large amounts of material were removed and cut at Dundanion to create part of the embankment there.

In addition, due to the fact that the construction was taking place during the Irish Great Famine, there was no shortage of labour. Huge numbers of unemployed people were attracted to the construction areas. In fact, trouble arose on more than one occasion with people who did not get jobs. For example, on 21 June 1847, seventy out of 2,000 men were hired. A week later, 600 of those who did not get a job invaded the site. A total of 450 men were taken on for the erection of the embankment at the Cork end of the line, and another eighty employed on digging the cutting beyond Blackrock.

During the entire construction period, there were only four fatalities. One man was killed by a spoil wagon, which knocked him down. Three were killed by the collapse of embankment. On 27 April 1850, the first trial run of a locomotive took place. The six-and-half-mile trip from Passage to Cork took 17 minutes. A week later, a second trial took place, this time from the city end of the line.

The official test run was shown in the *Illustrated London News*, on 25 May 1850. An engine pulled a first-class carriage, which carried the directors of Cork, Blackrock and Passage Railway and a group of merchants. The outward journey took 17 minutes and lasted just over 10 minutes on return. The line was opened to the public on Saturday 8 June 1850, and there was a service of ten trains each way at regular intervals. The departures from Cork to Passage were on the hour while those from Passage to the city were every half an hour.

In addition, the gradient of the line was fortunately small, with the highest point being approximately 7m above sea level and located just after the Blackrock Station. Cast-iron rails were used initially and replaced in 1890 with steel rails. William Dargan, a successful Irish railway contractor, was employed to complete the final section of the line between Toureen Strand and the Steam Packet Quay at Passage. The entire length of track between Cork and Passage was in place by April 1850, and within two months the line was opened for passenger traffic.

The original city terminus was located at Victoria Road. It was a two-storey structure with a corrugated iron roof in three parts, a centre and two sides. Cast-iron columns, manufactured by King Street Iron Works, supported the roof. However, in 1849, a year before the station opened, the local press began to complain about the station's location within the city. They argued that the site would interfere with future dock development in Monerea Marshes. The line near the station occupied a large area of river frontage, which the Harbour Board and Cork Corporation became more and more interested in acquiring.

The location problem was only rectified in the Cork Improvement Act of 1868 and in 1872. It was proposed to create a 2km diversion from the metal over-bridge on the Marina, which was to lead the line away from the riverfront along the Monerea marshes to a new terminus west of the City Park Station at Albert Road. This cost was paid for by Cork Corporation. Designed by John Benson, the new Cork terminus of

Test run of Cork, Blackrock and Passage Railway, 1850 from *Illustrated London News* (source: Cork City Library)

the Cork, Blackrock and Passage Railway's was opened and completed in 1873. The building is now marked by Long Construction services on Hibernian Road. Three new engines along with fifteen passenger carriages were bought from the Sharp brothers of Manchester.

In the late 1800s, the Cork, Blackrock and Passage Railway also operated a fleet of river steamers in competition with the River Steamer Company (RSC). The railway company expanded its fleet in 1881 but it was only when the service was extended to Aghada that profits grew. Steamers left Patrick's Bridge to stop at places such as Passage, Glenbrook, Monkstown, Ringaskiddy, Haulbowline, Queenstown and Aghada, Spike Island, and Curraghbinny.

In 1896, an Act of Parliament enabled the company to extend the line as far as Crosshaven. John Best Leith, Scotland, received the contract for the gauging of the line and works began in 1897. A new double track was laid between Cork and Blackrock, the only example of a double track in Ireland at the time. Unfortunately, by 1932 the increase in the use of motor cars had caused a decrease in the use of the line by passengers. Consequently, the railway was forced to close. Traces of the Cork, Blackrock and Passage Railway line, along a pedestrian walkway with several platforms, buildings and the steel viaduct that crossed the Douglas estuary, are still in public view.

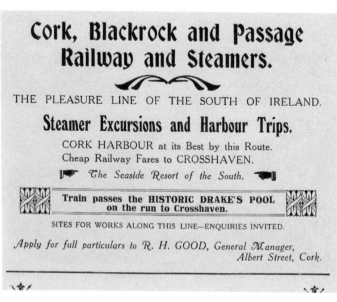

Advertisement for cross-harbour steamers, *c.*1916 (source: Cork City Library)

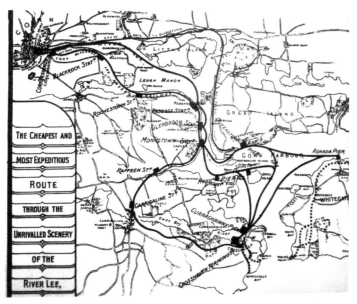

Railway map for cross-harbour connections, *c*.1910 (source: Cork City Library)

Cork, Youghal and Queenstown Railway

Between 1854 and 1862, a rail link was built between Cork and Youghal. It was supposed to be the western half of a proposed line between Waterford and Cork. The full line, though, was never constructed. Independent companies eventually completed the Waterford and Tramore section and the Cork–Youghal section. In the case of this latter section, work was sanctioned by Parliament in 1854 and a branch line to Queenstown was approved in 1845.

The first section of line to be constructed between Midleton and Dunkettle was awarded to Moores of Dublin, who proved problematic and was replaced by R.T. Carlisle of Canterbury. This line was opened in November 1859, having taken three years to complete. As a temporary measure, Cork-bound passengers continued their trip in a horse-drawn omnibus. By May 1860, the line had seen completed to Youghal, and to Tivoli in September. Eventually, in December 1861, the entire line was completed and first locomotive left Cork for Youghal.

The initial location of the proposed terminus was at the corner of St Patrick's Hill and MacCurtain Street, then known as King Street. The selected location, though, was at Summerhill, on a rock-cut ledge overlooking the Lower Glanmire Road. The terminus could accommodate two tracks, a simple station house, a goods shed and single passenger and goods platforms. Leaving Cork, the line ran parallel with Glanmire Road as far as Tivoli, where the road crossed over it. Access to important residences on the north side of line was also facilitated by three ornate cast-iron footbridges, which were supported on large brick columns. These still exist today. In addition, the Cork–Youghal line had ten locomotives. They were all built by Neilson and Company of Glasgow between 1859 and 1862.

In March 1862, the Queenstown branch opened but the profits were hindered by financial problems. Eventually, the railway was sold to the Great Southern and Western Railway in 1865 for £310,000. Hence, from 1868 onwards, the Cork, Youghal and Queenstown line could be taken at Penrose Quay.

Until 1877, a direct route could be taken from Queenstown to Dublin-Kingsbridge. The Summerhill station closed in 1893, and in February 1963 passenger services to Cork and Youghal discontinued. In 1992, Iarnród Éireann began to remove the rails on certain sections of the Cork–Youghal line. In recent years, the Cork–Midleton line and Cork–Cobh line has been re-established.

The Haulbowline Bridge

In October 1968, the opening of the new double bridge connected Haulbowline with the mainland at Ringaskiddy. For years previously, the only link with Ringaskiddy was a flimsy wooden pier, which became unusable after years of neglect and decay. Work in the steel works of Haulbowline factory depended on river ferries from Cobh or Monkstown, which naturally consumed time every day. Arrival at Ringaskiddy meant a further journey by car or by bicycle to the workers' homes. It was hoped that the bridge would encourage the construction of more houses, industrial developments and other amenities for the daily workers near Haulbowline.

Connected to Nature

In 2014, the Beaufort Research and Coastal and Marine Research Centre created a management and adaptation strategy for Cork Harbour. There is a significant section in their report on the natural heritage of the inner harbour and why it should get international recognition for the largest number of wintering birds on the east and south-east Irish coast, 20,000 waders and 5,000 wildfowl. The area is designated as Special Protection Area (SPA) and Ramsar Site for wetland protection with 1,436ha of designated area. The report notes: The area is an important site in Ireland for breeding common tern (*Sterna hirundo*) and for wintering great crested grebe (*Podiceps cristatus*), red-breasted merganser (*Mergus serrator*), oystercatcher (*Haematopus ostralegus*) and lapwing (*Vanellus vanellus*). Furthermore, the harbour supports whimbrel (*Numenius phaeopus*) and other species of national importance, including cormorant (*Phalacrocorax carbo*), common shelduck (*Tadorna tadorna*), wigeon (*Anas penelope*), teal (*Anas crecca*) and golden plover (*Pluvialis apricaria*)'.

In other areas of the harbour, visitors can view Cuskinny Nature Reserve, near Cobh. The land is owned by the Bird and Ronan families and comprises about 12ha of land located along the lower reaches of the Ballyleary Stream on the Great Island in Cork Harbour. It is managed by BirdWatch Ireland. Elsewhere, Harper's Island Wetland Centre is enjoying ongoing development and is currently owned by Cork County Council. It is managed in partnership with BirdWatch Ireland and the Glounthaune Community Association/Tidy Towns.

8

TALES OF SHIPPING

A Harbour of Shipwrecks

There are over 400 shipwrecks in Cork Harbour, ranging from seventeenth-century galleons to twentieth-century submarines. The locations of the majority of the 400, though, are unrecorded. Ireland's Underwater Archaeology Unit (UAU) was established within the National Monuments Service to manage and protect Ireland's underwater cultural heritage. The unit is engaged in the compilation of an inventory of shipwrecks recorded in Irish waters. The Shipwreck Inventory of Ireland includes all known wrecks for the years up to and including 1945, and approximately 12,000 records have been compiled and integrated into the shipwreck database thus far.

Drake's Pool

An eighteenth-century visitor to the Carrigaline area was Dr Charles Smith, who compiled a history of Cork (published in 1750). In his book is the first mention of the story concerning English Admiral Francis Drake. He wrote that Sir Francis Drake, in 1589 with a small squadron of five ships of war, was chased into Cork harbour by a fleet of Spanish galleons. He sailed into Crosshaven and moored his ships behind the shelter of Currabinny Hill in a safe basin. The Spaniards sailed up the harbour of Cork and were surprised not to see the ships they had just pursued. Hence having missed their prey, they came out again. Charles Smith refers to the hiding place as Drake's Pool. The name was supplied by later writers. It is not mentioned in any source previous to 1750, or in the accounts of Drake's movements.

Raleigh's Last Voyage

On 9 August 1617, English Captain Walter Raleigh sailed from Cork Harbour to the West Indies, and on his return was made a prisoner, lodged in the Tower of London, and ultimately beheaded there as an alleged traitor.

Piracy Annoyances
In a letter dated 13 September 1636, Lord Lieutenant Strafford wrote of piracy: 'The Turks still annoy this coast. They came of late into Cork Harbour, took a boat, which had eight fishermen in her, and gave chase to two more, who saved themselves among the rocks, the townsmen looking on at the same without means or power to assist them.'

Sunk by Gunpowder
The seventy-two-gun, third-rate gunship *Breda* was built by Betts in 1679 at Harwich. On 12 October 1690, she was anchored at Spike Island with a full complement of 400 aboard, including troops and 160 Jacobite prisoners, when a gunpowder explosion occurred. She took fire and blew up. Captain Barret, who escaped, was considered to have caused the explosion maliciously. There were nine other survivors.

Marauders in Disguise
In the 1720s, a small French privateer ship came and anchored off the town of Cove, under English colours. There were several English and Irish sailors amongst the crew, and all who were French carefully concealed themselves. The custom house officers came on board and were invited into the cabin, where they were plied with good French claret. However, the French crew detached themselves from the rest. There were two ships in the harbour, and most of their men were on shore. The Frenchmen had but one boat; but as soon as the tide began to ebb they made for the English customs officers' ships. They manned them both, trapped the crew, hoisted French colours on their own, and sailed off in triumph. When they were out of the harbour's mouth they stripped the officers naked and sent them adrift in their own boat.

A Great Transhipment Centre
Having accommodated the British Navy throughout the eighteenth century, Cork port was capable of facilitating the emigration process. From the middle of the century, more people left from the port of Cork than any other Irish harbour. It became more important than the traditional emigration ports of the north: Londonderry and Belfast. By 1867, more Irish people were leaving Cork than the great transhipment centre of the world – Liverpool. The motives for such departure were multifaceted.

The Cornwallis Convoy
On 6 January 1776, HMS *Bristol* arrived in Cove as part of a convoy taking troops to America under Lord Cornwallis to fight in the American War of Independence campaign. The HMS *Bristol* was a ship of 1,049 tons; she was 146ft long on her upper gundeck and was

40ft 7in wide across the beam. She was armed with twenty-two 24-powder long guns on her lower gundeck, twenty-two 12-powder long guns on her upper gundeck, four 6-powder long guns on her quarterdeck with two more on her forecastle. She was manned by a crew of 350 men, officers, boys and marines.

Sunk by a Rat

On 17 September 1776 the vessel *Henrietta*, under Captain Bastable, was journeying to Cove within Cork Harbour with passengers and merchant goods. The *Freeman's Journal* records that she was sank due to a leak in her bottom caused by a rat hole.

Deepening the Channel

During the winter of 1789 and the spring of 1790, the depth of the channel from Blackrock to the city was deepened from 6 to 7ft. Prior to the deepening, ships of 300 tons could not come up to load and unload at the quays. Two hundred lighters transported goods regularly into the city's quays but this number, through the deepening, was reduced to ten to fifteen.

Dragged by a Hurricane

The French brig *Suffisante* was apprehended at Texel, Netherlands, on 31 August 1795 and relocated to the British Royal Navy. On 27 September 1803, the brig sailed from Cove under Captain Heathcoate, transporting a number of volunteer seamen and soldiers for England. She dragged her anchors during a hurricane, struck on Spike Island and collapsed over on her beam end. Seven of the crew drowned and three were killed by a falling mast. The vessel went to pieces. In 1980, dredging work on the bar and channel around the Spit raised a large quantity of her wreckage, some of which was placed in Cobh museum for public display.

Cork Harbour Commissioners

Cork Harbour Commissioners were established in 1813 and they focussed their work on the improvement, management and maintenance of the shipping channels and city's quays. During the following decades the Commissioners tackled a wide agenda of repairing and rebuilding the quays in limestone ashlar construction and this comprised the insertion of '8,000 timber toe piles' driven to depths of 21ft in order to enable dredging adjacent to the quays. The Commissioners spent a total of £34,389, raised from harbour fees, between 1827 and 1834 on the improvement of the city quays. Once the quays were in a stable condition, the river channels were extensively dredged and the extracted material was used to reclaim areas of slobland, including the City Park area behind the Navigation Wall. Timber wharfs began to be constructed along a number of the quays in the second half of the nineteenth century, including Albert, Union, Victoria, St Patrick's and Penrose Quays. In 1874, timber wharves were added to the south jetties. There were seven jetties constructed, each 43 1/2ft wide and initially separated by 120 ft of clear space, which were subsequently filled in.

Commuting the Lee
On 10 June 1815, the *City of Cork* steamer was launched at Passage, the first steamer that plied on the Lee connecting Cove with Cork.

Surprise!
On 8 May 1816, thirty convicts from Tipperary and other counties were sent down from Cork City Gaol and put on board the transports at Cove. There a hulk called the *Surprise* was stationed for many years, in which convicts were detained until the ships were ready to take them out to Botany Bay and other penal settlements in Australia.

On 1 August 1823, the convict ships *Isabella*, *Medina*, and *Castle Forbes* were expected in the harbour in order to take 520 male convicts to New South Wales. There were 350 convicts in the City and in the *Surprise*, at Cove, a further 300, making a total of 650 who needed to be trans-shipped. Of these, about 100 had been convicted under the Insurrection Act.

The Souvenir of the Mary Russell
In 1828, the Cork Harbour authorities boarded a schooner called the *Mary Russell*, which arrived in the harbour. On boarding her it was discovered that the crew had been murdered by the captain a few days previously. The master, Captain Stewart, and the cabin boy survived the onslaught.

On being tried Captain Stewart was pronounced as 'insane' at the time of his crime. He was sentenced to the Asylum for Criminal Lunatics at Dundrum (Co. Dublin). Soon after the patient was transferred to the Cork District Asylum at the request of Dr Thomas Carey Osburne.

During his stay in Cork, Captain Stewart suffered several attacks of homicidal mania. Between these outbreaks though, he was perfectly natural, and a very friendly person. In the Cork institution he gathered the left-over beef and mutton bones after the patients' meals, and with these he created a little ship. He used very hard bone to carve the decorations of the vessel. When finished, he presented it to his medical attendant, Dr Osburne. In time Captain Stewart was transferred to Dundrum Asylum for Criminal Lunatics, where he remained until his death in August 1878.

Wheeler's Ship Yard

There has been a ship-building concern in Rushbrooke since the nineteenth century. Joseph Wheeler was one of a group of enterprising Cork businessmen who initially financed the shipbuilding industry in Cork Harbour. The period 1832–60 was particularly prosperous in Cork's shipping history and the house flags of many of Cork's shipping firms were to be seen on the masts of their vessels in all parts of the world. There were the shipyards of Hennessy and Brown at Passage West and those of Wheeler, Pike and Robinson at the head of the river. Numerous timber and iron ships were produced for home and foreign owners – ships which conformed to the highest international standards of the time and enhanced the reputation of Cork Harbour's craftsmen. In around the 1840s, Joseph Wheeler also had a building slip on the Cork riverbank. The *Cork Directory* of 1842–43 contains the following entry: *Joseph Wheeler, Ship-builder*. His shipyard was located near where the Port of Cork yard now stands. Wheeler built numerous timber vessels for Cork-based owners and foreign merchants. The *Illustrated London News* of 11 February 1860 carried a description of a 500-ton sailing ship from Wheeler's Yard. The *Aura* was the largest ship to be constructed in Cork up to that date. She was the eighth vessel to be built for exporter Mr Harvey and was to be commanded by Corkman and seaman Captain Belchel.

Wheeler's enterprise at Rushbrooke opened for shipbuilding in 1860. Between 1917 and 1920, the dock, then owned by the Furness Whithy Company, was enlarged. While no ships were built at Rushbrooke – with the exception of some 200-ton barges – very extensive alterations were undertaken, and in some major overhauls ships were almost literally rebuilt there. In the post-war years, when the Cork Dockyard operated the yard, major conversion work was successfully done at Rushbrooke including the conversion of two ex-Flower Class corvettes to passenger and cargo vessels for Mediterranean service and the conversion of an ex-River Class frigate to a passenger and motor car ferry for the Dover–Calais service. In the late 1950s, Verolme Dockyard was developed on the site (see Chapter 9).

The End of the Hulk

In early November 1836, the *Hulk at* Haulbowline was a ship like the *Surprise*, for the reception of felons under sentence of transportation. However, under new prison regulations, the prisoners who were confined in the *Hulk* were to be turned over to the city and county gaols – the new place of exportation to Australia was to be in Kingstown.

A Sirius Point

Perhaps the most famous steamship acquired by the City of Cork Steamship Company was the *Sirius*. Built in 1837 by Menzies & Co., Perth and engineered by J. Wingate & Co, Glasgow at a cost of £27,000. The dog figurehead was named after the dog star Sirius. The vessel will be remembered for being the first passenger steamship to make the voyage from Europe to America, from London via Cork to New York. On 28 March 1838, the *Sirius* began her journey from London to New York. She stopped at Cork to load up on coal and embark mail and passengers.

The *Ocean* steamship arrived from Liverpool on 3 April with mail and passengers. Next morning at 10 a.m., the *Sirius* got under way, being accompanied as far the entrance to the harbour by the *Ocean*. A brief stoppage was made while the *Ocean* went alongside the *Sirius* to bring off a number of ladies and gentlemen who had been permitted to accompany their friends to the harbour mouth. The steamers exchanged salutes and then the *Sirius* continued on her course.

The ship arrived in New York at 10 p.m. on 20 April. The *Sirius* was to make two further transatlantic voyages and afterwards returned to the home and continental services.

Arrival of the "Sirius" at New York, 22nd April, 1838.

Depiction of *Sirius*, 1847 (source: Cork City Library)

The *Sirius* became the property of the Cork Steamship Company and was employed in the Glasgow, Dublin and Cork Service until 1847, when disaster struck. On the evening of 15 June 1847, the ship sailed from Dublin to Cork with a general cargo and forty passengers. Everything was well until 4 a.m. on 16 June when she encountered a dense fog and went onto the rocks in Ballycotton Bay. Twelve passengers and two seamen were drowned by the capsizing of one of the launch boats. The rest of the passengers and crew were saved by means of a rope, which was passed from the ship to the shore. The vessel went to pieces by 22 June.

A Voyage of Relief

On 3 March 1847, by a joint resolution of both American Houses, the President and Secretary of the Navy were authorised to send the frigate *Macedonian* and the sloop of war *Jamestown*, vessels at the expense of the United States, and to put them into the hands of Captains de Kay and Forbes, respectively, for the benevolent purpose of providing food aid for Ireland during the Great Famine.

The *Jamestown* was a sloop of war, one of six owned by the US government. It was built in Norfolk, Virginia, in 1843. Her armament consisted of twenty-two guns in all. All but two guns were removed, and the order for the delivery of the *Jamestown* with 8,000 barrels' bulk of provisions, grain, meal, etc. was given to Captain Forbes. On arrival in Cork, the steamship SS *Sabrina* took the *Jameson* in tow and placed her near the Government Stores Haulbowline.

In 1880, the American government sent over another ship to Cork Harbour. Named the *Constellation*, she was sent to provide food to impoverished people in the west of Ireland.

An Emigrant Hub

In 1846–47, considering all ports in the United Kingdom, Cork was surpassed in emigration numbers only by Liverpool. Approximately 17,000 individuals travelled on an Atlantic crossing via Cork City port in 1847. At the height of the famine, 5,000 men, women and children left Cork City each week.

The Eastern Europe Connection

In about the year 1850, following the Repeal of the Corn Laws, ships laden with corn, mostly from the Black Sea and the Danube, began to call in Cork Harbour for orders, often arriving in large fleets. These ships continued to arrive until towards the close of the nineteenth century, when the introduction of cargo steamers of much larger

Emigration from Queenstown, 1874 from *Illustrated London News* (source: Cork City Library)

carrying capacity, and going direct to their ports of discharge, put an end to these sailing ships coming to Cork.

The Upper and Lower Harbour Distribution

Figures distinguishing the upper and lower harbour only started to be accumulated in May 1851 in British Parliamentary Papers. From May 1851 to the end of 1855, more than 104,000 emigrants left Cork City, while during the same period 28,000 departed Queenstown – the volume of migration from the city was four times greater than the lower harbour. Considering 1855 in isolation, some 97 per cent of emigrants sailed from the upper harbour.

A Deep Water Pier

In 1853, the Commissioners were granted permission by the Secretary of the Admiralty to proceed with a deep water pier at Queenstown. Although a pier already existed there, a deep-water facility was necessary. However, plans for its construction faltered. Over a decade, later the Harbour Board appointed a committee to bring to the notice of Parliament the advantage that such a pier would bring for both government and passenger purposes.

Queensland Bound

In the years 1861, 1863 and 1866, several large sailing vessels left Queenstown transporting a considerable number of emigrants, free or assisted, to Queensland, Australia, including some natives of the town. Queensland was a penal colony established in 1824. Penal transportation ceased in 1839 and free settlement was allowed from 1842.

An Intoxication Case

In 1852, the 223-ton brig *Hannah* was 2 years old. She was en route from Queenstown to Newry with nine crew members and a cargo of Indian corn. She encountered a NW force 5 wind with squally conditions and went ashore while leaving the harbour on 27 October 1852. This is thought to have been caused by the pilot being intoxicated. The master was also blamed for allowing such a person to take charge of his vessel. The estimated loss on the vessel was £1,500.

The Advent of Cunard

On 6 November 1859, the Cunard paddle steamer named *Canada* steamed into Cobh harbour, beginning a connection between Cobh and North America. The connection continued without interruption except during the periods of the two world wars. Built in 1848, the *Canada* was a tiny wooden paddle steamer of 1,831 gross tons. She used sail as well as her side-lever engines to cross the Atlantic.

Cobh saw the development in size, speed and comfort of the Cunard transatlantic liners from wooden paddle steamer to quadruple-screw, 1.000ft liner.

The history of Cunard over the ensuing century from 1859 was woven with the history of Cobh itself. Many of the population worked with the company. The people of the town have watched the arrivals of new ships of the fleet or bade farewell to the old. Cunard's association with Cobh is so much a part of Irish history. Many an Irish emigrant used the line as the first step to seek their fortune in North America. Great improvements were made by the Cork Harbour Board, with port facilities and lighting and buoying of the entire area under the control of that ever-watchful board.

The *Servia* was built in Glasgow in 1881 and was the first Cunard liner to be built of steel. The 7,392-ton vessel was the first ship to be lit by electricity and could exceed 16 knots. Over 1,000 passengers were carried on board. The *Servia* regularly called at Queenstown from 1881 to 1901. The ship plied the Liverpool–Queenstown–New York route until required for troop transport duties during the Anglo–Boer War. In November 1899, the *Servia* docked beside Queenstown railway station and took on board 1,500 troops, ammunition, stores,

Cunard Liner at Queenstown by Robert Lowe Stopford, late nineteenth
century (source: Cork City Library)

baggage and horses. The model of the *Servia* in the Cobh Heritage
Centre was constructed for the 1992 film *Far and Away*, starring Tom
Cruise and Nicole Kidman.

Among the Cunarders, which maintained the company's services
between Ireland and the United States and Canada in 1959, were
the 27,778-ton *Britannic*, one of the world's largest liners, and the
35,055-ton *Mauretania*. Periodically calling at Cobh, too, were the four
sleek 22,000-ton sisters of the Canadian service, the *Saxonia*, *Ivernia*,
Canntma and *Sylvania*.

In 1960, the Cunard liners plying from Liverpool, London and
Southampton to the United States and Canada made a total of sixty-
nine westbound and eastbound calls at Cobh.

Regular visitors to Cobh during the season were the *Mauretania* and
Britannic, en route to and from New York, and the *Saxonia* and *Ivernia*
bound for Quebec and Montreal.

During the winter months the Liverpool-based *Carinthia* and
Sylvania called at Cobh on voyages in the Liverpool–Halifax–New
York service.

For many years, one of the surest advance indications of the
approaching Christmas season was the annual visit by one of the cargo
liners of the Cunard Steamship Company with dried fruit and such

ships as the *Bosnia*, *Bothnia*, *Bantria*, and *Bresci*, as well as many others, all berthed in Cork on different occasions.

The Inman Pier

In November 1872, the Inman line submitted plans for a 600ft quay with jetties to be built at the east end of Queenstown. The plans were referred to the pilot committee, who visited the proposed site and rejected the application on the grounds that it should be a public facility. Nevertheless, the construction began, but the Inman Line was unable to extend it as far eastwards as they wished, without the board's sanction.

Fleets and Lines

In 1881, Queenstown accounted for 90 per cent of emigration from Cork port while the city's quays absorbed approximately 3,500 passengers from a total of 36,000. The port of Cork's contribution to the national sum of emigration was 46 per cent. By 1881, no fewer than ten steam companies were calling at Liverpool to convey passengers, of which nine stopped at Queenstown: the Allan Line, the American Line, the Beaver Line, the Cunard Line, the Dominion Line, the Inman Line, the Guion Line, the National Line and the White Star Line. The Warren Line was the only company that did not make Queenstown a port of call.

The advent of the twentieth century coincided with new challenges. Queenstown's position as a gateway of departure was threatened before the era was a decade old. In 1907, the White Star Line changed its terminal from Liverpool to Southampton and bypassed Queenstown as a port of call on its eastbound route.

Eyes on the Blue Riband Award

The Blue Riband was the symbolic honour awarded to the passenger steamship which made the fastest crossing of the North Atlantic. Until the First World War, Daunt's Rock, outside Cork harbour, was the measuring point at which a liner on the Liverpool–New York run was judged to have begun or finished a crossing.

The tradition of tea clipper ships racing against each other was carried into the age of steam, when comparisons were made of the length of time taken to cross the Atlantic.

The term Blue Riband does not seem to have been used in the first days of steam when the first Cunarders mobilised the crossing. From the 1850s until 1897, the Blue Riband was claimed by ships of four British companies: the Cunard, Inman, White Star and Guion Lines.

Between 1897 and 1907, the Blue Riband holders were German

owned and did not call at Queenstown. In 1907, Cunard's new *Lusitania* and *Mauretania* brought the record back to Daunt's Rock. After the First World War, Cunard moved its express service to Southampton and replaced the Queenstown call with Cherbourg. Bishop's Rock, off Cornwall, permanently replaced Daunt's Rock as the measuring post, and Queenstown's Blue Riband connection passed into history.

To Save the Helga

On the stretch of coastline east of Cork Harbour, extending from Poer Head to Ballycotton, there foundered the ships *Helga*, *Saga*, *Ibis*, *Sirius*, *Cellestina*, *Euphinia*, *Cooleen*, to mention but a few of the many vessels that found watery graves on that short stretch of coastline.

In 1903, the *Helga* was a London ship of 1,668 tons. She was bound from San Francisco to Queenstown with a cargo of wheat for the company Halls of Cork. She was manned by a crew of twenty-three under the command of a Captain Ferguson. After 140 days at sea, the *Helga* arrived off the English coast. Weather conditions were not good as they headed for Cork Harbour. On arrival, the ship put under small sail hoping to get a pilot. To attract attention, they burned signals of blue lights and flare-up lights. The wind was blowing from the south-east. They hugged the shore in case the wind should shift north and carry them off land. At 3 a.m. there was no easing of the gale. The crew tacked ship and hauled up the foresail. Some of the crew who were up the rigging were ordered back on deck by the captain. The tide was carrying the ship towards the shore.

The lifeboats were launched but before anybody had climbed in, the *Helga* struck sand bottom, and seemed to scrape as she drove towards the shore. The captain's wife was the first into a lifeboat, and was followed by others. It was raining heavily. It was no longer possible to see the shore. All the crew and captain got safely into their boats, leaving on board the ship's three dogs and a pig to meet their fate. Having sent up signals, they anxiously awaited help.

Two coastguard boats came to the assistance of the *Helga* crew, as well as a Liverpool tug *Blazer* and the Cork Harbour screw-tug *Mayflower*. They picked up the crew and took them into Queenstown, cold, wet, and hungry, as they were.

Efforts were made to refloat the *Helga*. The tugs *Flying Fox*, *Flying Sportsman* and *Mayflower* were used without success. When the crew went on board to collect some of the belongings from the *Helga*, they found that the cabins had been looted, and clothes, tobacco, cigars and other articles had been removed from the ship.

Titanic *Heritage*

Cobh's Queenstown Story and the *Titanic* Experience recall in great depth the day the RMS *Titanic* had in this harbour town in 1912. The White Star Line pier is the same structure that supported the 123 *Titanic* passengers who embarked on that fateful voyage in April 1912. Some made the journey in groups, travelling with relatives, neighbours or friends. Ames Flynn was one of a group of fourteen leaving the Addergoole area of Athlone, County Westmeath. Emigrant Dannie Buckley joined four others from Kingwilliamstown (now Ballydesmond), County Cork, while Ellen Mockler was one of five people leaving Caltra, County Galway. Six members of the Rice family, widow Margaret and her five sons, were returning to Spokane, Washington, from Athlone, County Westmeath.

The *Titanic* pier is also symbolic for the thousands of Irish emigrants who departed from the town of Cobh to build new lives abroad and in the USA. The Centenary Anniversary Commemoration of the sinking of the *Titanic* took place in 2012, and ongoing lobbying of local and national government is still taking place to secure the future of the pier. *Titanic* Experience Cobh is a visitor attraction, which is located in the original offices of the White Star Line.

From Titanic, Goodbye All

Jeremiah Burke, 19, from Glanmire in Cork was given a small bottle at the quayside in Cobh by his mother before he set off for the USA on the *Titanic*. As the ship sank in the early hours of 15 April 1912, he threw the bottle and message into the sea. The bottle was washed ashore a year later in Dunkettle, only a few miles from his family home. The note, which read 'From *Titanic*, goodbye all, Burke of Glanmire, Cork' has remained in the Burke family for nearly a century. One of Jeremiah's nieces, Mary Woods, donated it to the Cobh Heritage Centre.

Lusitania

On 7 May 1915, the ship *Lusitania* was torpedoed by a German U-boat off Cork Harbour and the Old Head of Kinsale. Survivors were taken from the water and from lifeboats to the Cunard Line offices. The base for the rescue operations, which comprised local fishermen and naval personnel, was also carried out from Queenstown (now Cobh). A monument in Cobh by Irish–American sculptor of note Jerome Connor was unveiled in 1968. Seamus Murphy was responsible for the stone carvings. To underline the importance of the local fishermen in rescuing the survivors, two of them are depicted in the memorial below the so-called Angel of Peace. The Lusitania Peace Memorial Committee included Franklin D. Roosevelt, Gertrude Vanderbilt and leading public figures.

The Scuttling of the Aud

Perhaps one of the best famous boats remembered in Irish history, the *Aud*, was originally called the SS *Libau*. It was constructed in 1907 for the Wilson Shipping Company of Hull in England. Its purpose was as a steam cargo transport ship. During the First World War it was renamed the SS *Castro* and and was seized by the German Navy in the Kiel Canal.

In the lead up to the Irish Easter Rising in Dublin in 1916, a plan was put in place by Irish Volunteers to convey through the SS *Castro* three machine guns, 20,000 rifles and one million rounds of ammunition to the Rising participants. The ship was disguised as a Norwegian steamer and renamed the *Aud*.

On 20 April 1916, the *Aud* arrived off the Kerry coast but failed to land its cargo in Fenit Harbour. The *Aud* had been followed by the Royal Navy for its entire journey to Ireland.

The ship was captured by the British and taken to Cork Harbour for lock-up. However, on 22 April 1916, to avoid the ship and its contents falling into the hands of the enemy. the captain of the vessel, Karl Spindler, scuttled the ship near the harbour, 2 miles east of Daunt Rock Lightship.

Sir Roger Casement, who had arranged the arms shipment with Germany, came by German U-Boat to Banna Strand believing that the plan was solid and that he would meet the *Aud* and begin the distribution of weapons. He was subsequently apprehended, tried for treason and put to death on 3 August 1916.

UC-42, Mine Layer

During an inspection of pipelines to the Kinsale gas field in November 2010, a German U-boat *UC-42* was found. It is reputed that in 1917 this U-boat was laying mines at the entrance to Cork Harbour. After possibly detonating one of its own mines, it sank with twenty-seven crew lost.

The American Presence

Immediately following the declaration of war by the USA on 6 April 1917, a force of destroyers of the US Navy set sail for Cork Harbour, arriving there on 4 May. At that time, the Naval Aviation Command was still in its infancy and not quite prepared for the task ahead. A total of twenty-five air stations were eventually established throughout Europe, five of which were to be in Ireland. All the US Navy's seaplanes were shipped to Ireland in crates and taken to Aghada for assembly before delivery to their assigned stations. Aghada also became the main training base where all aircrew training was conducted. A further vital role for Aghada was as a patrol base, searching for German U-boats from Cape Clear eastwards into St George's Channel. But some thirteen weeks after the first flight out of Aghada, the Armistice was signed on 11 November 1918, bringing patrols to an end. Production of aircraft, which had peaked at one completed every three days, came to a halt and the forty-eight officers and 1,398 men began leaving Aghada.

The Doom of the Celtic
The White Star liner *Celtic*, 21,179 tons gross, left New York on 1 December 1928 for Liverpool. She sank off Roche's Point, on 10 December. Her 260 passengers, who included twenty-seven survivors of the *Vestris* disaster, were placed on tenders, and landed at Queenstown at noon. A southerly gale, accompanied by high seas, was raging at 3.30 a.m. when the *Celtic* lay outside the harbour awaiting the arrival of Mr C. O'Donovan, the White Star Line's special pilot, but owing to the weather the pilot boat was unable to approach the vessel. At 4.30 a.m. the *Celtic* came in closer, and the first news of anything untoward was the sounding of six blasts upon the liner's siren.

Shortly afterwards, a telephone message from Roche's Point was received at Queenstown, conveying the news that the *Celtic* was ashore on a rock, known as Calf's Rock, near the lighthouse and required immediate assistance. The Dutch tug *Gelezee* and the local tug *Morsecock* immediately responded, and got hawser cables aboard the stranded vessel. For hours, the tugs struggled to get the liner into deep water, but without success. At low tide the *Celtic* was virtually high and dry about 30 yards from Calf's Rock, and lying parallel to the mainland, 300 yards distant. Towage operations were resumed, but without success. The captain, with a skeleton crew, remained on board, but was unable to render much assistance as the *Celtic*'s boilers were out of commission.

Keep All Who Travel In Her
The end of the Second World War led to new engineering opportunities for ship owners. On Friday 12 December 1947, Mrs F.P. Hallinan, wife of the Chairman of the Cork Harbour Commissioners, launched the new MV *Innisfallen* for the Cork–Fishguard service at Dunbarton. She noted: 'I name this ship *Innisfallen*; may God care and keep all who travel in her.' A bottle of champagne then hit the bow of the new vessel, with the tricolour on the foremast.

According to the *Cork Examiner*, the new passenger-cargo vessel had been built at the yards of Messrs Denny and Brothers, Ltd, Dumbarton, Firth of Clyde, for the British and Irish Steampacket Company, which operated the City of Cork Steam Packet Company (1936) Ltd. This was the third *Innisfallen*. Her predecessor sunk at the mouth of the Mersey in 1940 after she had given excellent service between Cork and Fishguard for over ten years. The first *Innisfallen* was lost during the Second World War. The new vessel was built expressly for the direct Cork–Fishguard service. She took up her station in the early summer of 1948, a thrice-weekly run in each direction. A unique feature of the new vessel was a stabiliser, which would prevent rolling in bad weather. This would be the first vessel running between Britain and Ireland to have one. However, the Second World War caused more than the loss of B & I vessels – it hastened developments in ship construction and aids to mariners. One of the most important of these was radar, which the new vessel possessed.

The new *Innisfallen* had a green-coloured hull and cream upper works, departing from the old black and white colour scheme of the City of Cork Steam Packet Company. The *Innisfallen* had accommodation for 950 passengers, with first-class berths for 193 passengers and third-class berths for sixty passengers. The cargo capacity was approximately 700 tons, and for the conveyance of perishable goods there was refrigeration between decks aft, plus space for the conveyance of motor cars aft. Another feature of the design was that in the lounge and smoke room the lighting and ventilation fittings were combined, leading to a simplification of the architectural treatment of the ceilings. In the deluxe cabins and the forward sections of the first-class accommodation, thermostat control was installed for individual adjustment of room temperature.

Severin's St Brendan's Voyage

A specialist in medieval travel, Tim Severin is best known in Ireland as the man who, with chosen companions, sailed a 36ft leather-skinned boat from Ireland to Newfoundland via Iceland in 1976–77 to demonstrate that Irish monks, most probably led by St Brendan the Navigator, could have reached the New World before the Vikings and almost 1000 years before Christopher Columbus. His leather-skinned boat, *St Brendan*, was built in Crosshaven. It first took to the water there and, after trials and testing, it sailed from Brandon Creek in County Kerry.

Around the World

Sir Francis Chichester (1901–72), was a pioneer aviator, explorer, author and racing enthusiast. Chichester attained global fame in the summer of 1967 when he finished an around the world solo trip in his yacht, the *Gipsy Moth IV*. His voyage achieved a new world circumnavigation record of 274 days for this 28,500-mile journey.

Chichester later built *Gipsy Moth V*, which he himself described as a 'most beautiful boat'. It was cast for him by the Irish firm Tonge & Taggart Ltd, and fitted out by Crosshaven Boat Yard. The precision keel was cast to exacting specifications, within limits of plus or minus 1/16th of an inch. In 1967, in the same boat, he set new speed records in single-handed sailing from West Africa to the Caribbean, a distance of 4,000 miles. While sailing *Gipsy Moth V* in the 1972 Transatlantic race, Chichester, weakened by cancer near his spine, had to abandon the race. Two months later he passed away.

Gipsy Moth V took part in races such as the Round Britain and East to West Transatlantic. In 1982, she was sailed in the first Around Alone race. Sailor Desmond Hampton borrowed her from the Chichester family but unfortunately ran the *Gipsy Moth V* aground on Gabo Island, near the north of Bass Strait, just off Australia's south-eastern coast.

The New Deep Water Terminal

Cunard Liner *Queen Elizabeth 2* (*QE2*) sailed into Cork Harbour for the first time on 20 July 1990. Circa 40,000 people thronged the piers of Ringaskiddy. The event marked a century and half of Cunard in business and also the official opening of a deep-water terminal in Cork Harbour. The port of Cork could now manage large-scale ocean liners the size of the *QE2*. The terminal was named after former Taoiseach of Ireland Seán Lemass. His daughter, Maureen Haughey, was present to do the honours of unveiling the plaque.

Tall Ships Race

In July 1991, the ninety-strong fleet involved in the 1,000-mile Tall Ships Race (or Cutty Sark Race) arrived at Cork Harbour, including *Asgard II* and seven other Irish ships. Ireland's President, Mary Robinson, joined thousands of spectators who lined the Cork waterfront to enjoy the show. Over 3,000 sailors from all over the world arrived in the maritime city by the Lee for the event.

A Naval Review

Irish History was made on 12 July 1996 when the first naval review was carried out in order to mark the fiftieth anniversary of the Irish Naval Service. The flagship LÉ *Eithne* hosted dignitaries such as President Mary Robinson, the Minister for Defence Seán Barrett and Flag Officer of the Naval Service Commodore John Kavanagh were present to review the lined-up fleet.

Seven ships of the Irish Naval Service were on display as well as those from eight additional visiting naval services, and a flotilla of small boats. In a display of Anglo–Irish relations, the ship's company of the Royal Navy's HMS *Manchester* completed a distinct salute for the President as she passed by.

Formation of the Port of Cork Company

Subsequent to the Harbours Act in 1996, all revalued assets of the Cork Harbour Commissioners were reinvested in the Port of Cork Company. The new company became a statutory authority responsible for the administration, regulation, running, and growth of the Port of Cork (in accordance with the Act). The Port of Cork company remains situated in the Custom House, Cork City.

Shipping for the Millennium

Near the turn of the twenty-first century, the Port of Cork was the second busiest port in Ireland in terms of the number of containers handled. The Port of Cork Company's annual reports highlight that the multitude of containers shipped through the port of Cork were bound to and from the mainland European ports of Rotterdam, Antwerp and Zeebrugee on services operated by BG Freightline, Eucon Shipping & Transport, Samskip, APL and X-press container line. Additionally, the Grimaldi-Euromed service offered weekly connections linking Ringaskiddy in Cork with Scandinavia, north–west Europe and the Mediterranean. The port continued to finance facilities and machinery at the Tivoli Container Terminal to guarantee that the high level of service for customers was upheld. Investment was injected into the Ringaskiddy Deepwater Terminal, with €3.6 million spent on new plant equipment to help meet customer needs and to increase efficiency at the Port of Cork.

  Of the total throughput at the Port of Cork, oil traffic accounted for near 60 per cent of cargo handled. The Port of Cork Company report for 2008 showcases that oil traffic 'decreased by 4.459 per cent to 5.8 million tonnes, the bulk of which is processed through Conoco Philips' Whitegate Oil Refinery. Non-oil accounted for 4.28 million tonnes in 2008, a decrease of 179,185 tonnes or 4.56 per cent when compared with the same period in 2007'. Whilst there was a reduction in container traffic, other cargoes such as cereals, coal, bulk fertiliser and animal feeds showed minor rises.

  The 2008 report also reveals that the port's facilities for the importation of trade cars are used by Ford, Opel, Fiat, Audi, Volkswagen, Mercedes-Benz, Peugeot, Citroen, Chrysler and Skoda, and Mazda: 'The number of vehicles handled in 2008 was 53,000 units, a decrease of 31.44 per cent over the same period in 2007.' Trade cars were handled at both Tivoli and Ringaskiddy. Today trade continues to build across the latter sectors described.

Port of Cork Future

In May 2015, the Port of Cork welcomed the decision of An Bord Pleanála to grant planning permission for the Ringaskiddy Port Redevelopment project in the lower harbour. The ensuing press release and newspaper spread detailed that development would amount to an investment of around €100 million. Such investment would create the finance base to extend the existing facilities that the port currently operates in Ringaskiddy.

The development also forms the first phase of the implementation of the Port of Cork's Strategic Development Plan Review (2010). The review sets out the key recommendations in the National Ports Policy, which highlights Cork as a Tier 1 port of national significance. Phase 1 of the Ringaskiddy Port Redevelopment project was expected to be operational in 2018–19. The overall project will enable, on a phased basis, the Port of Cork in transferring cargo handling activities from Tivoli and the City Quays in the future.

A Top Cruise Destination

In 2017, cruise ships calling at Irish ports range from the largest vessels operating in Europe, such as the *Royal Princess* with over 5,000 passengers and crew, to smaller expedition and luxury vessels with just fifty passengers. A total of sixty-five calls arrived in Cork Harbour, bringing approximately 160,000 passengers and crew to Cork city and county up until November. Cobh was voted as the second-best cruise destination in Western Europe.

International Missions

There are currently eight ships in the Irish Navy fleet, with one more under construction. At the headquarters of the Irish Navy on Haulbowline Island, the service maps out its activities from fishery protection and the seizure of narcotics and other illegal cargoes through routine patrols and intelligence-led operations. In press releases in 2015, three Irish Navy vessels were deployed consecutively to the Mediterranean to rescue migrants fleeing Africa in makeshift and unseaworthy vessels. The LÉ *Eithne* alone rescued 3,377 migrants before returning to Ireland. In the 48 hours of 28 and 29 June, she picked up 1,240 people. The LÉ *Niamh* rescued 3,014 people and the LÉ *Samuel Beckett* is currently deployed in the area.

9

THE INDUSTRIAL HARBOUR

The Port City and Tivoli

The modern river port of Cork City began to take shape about the middle of the eighteenth century. Consolidation of the marshy islands provided building space, and the covering over of the river channels and canals made wide streets possible. Quay walls were built at low-water level and could not accommodate ships of moderately heavy burden, which had to lighten cargo down the harbour for road transport to the city.

Following the constitution of the Cork Harbour Commissioners in 1813 and the introduction of steam dredging, a vigorous programme of river and berth deepening, quay and wharf building commenced. This and the introduction of the railways made the nineteenth century notable for development.

During and up to the early years of the twentieth century, berths were deepened at low water to keep all shipping afloat at lowest tides. Wharves and deep water quays were built. In 1919, the Cork Harbour Commissioners acquired from the Board of Trade 153 acres of slobland at Tivoli for the purpose of pumping dredged material ashore, thus creating new land for industrial purposes. This happened over several decades. In the early 1950s, oil storage depots were developed on the site. A further 10 acres were made available for development c.1960.

From 1960, modern Cork Harbour began to emerge, with the construction of oil terminals, steel mills, shipyards, a deep water ferry port and industrial base. The entire concept of transporting general cargo underwent radical changes with the introduction of containerisation. That brought about revolutionary changes in ports. Whereas previously the only requirements of general cargo services were quays and adjoining transit sheds, the ports now had to provide quays with high load-bearing qualities and wide aprons, specialised container cranes, large marshalling areas for containers and further specialised handling machinery within the container compounds.

Blackrock and Lough Mahon, by W.H. Bartlett, *c.*1841, from *The Scenery and Antiquities of Ireland* (source: Cork City Library)

At Tivoli Industrial and Dock Estate new facilities included new container, roll-on roll-off and conventional berths, a 30-ton gantry-type container crane, a modern transit shed, a passenger terminal and office block and an extensive paved area for the marshalling of containers and commercial vehicles. Thirty-seven acres were allocated for general cargo purposes.

Cork was the first port in Ireland to set up a planning and development department. By 1972, this produced the Cork Harbour Development Plan in which the blueprint was developed for a future that would include sites such as those at Ringaskiddy, Little Island, and Cobh. By the middle of the present decade, employment in these industries was predicted to exceed 5,000 people, and the port's frequent shipping services are an important factor in attracting new industries.

Douglas: The Sailcloth Factory

In the first half of the eighteenth century, the linen industry of Ireland was at its zenith and as a result numerous industries were started. One of these was the manufacture of sailcloth, a very necessary commodity of those times. In the year 1726, a Douglas factory embarked on the making of sailcloth. Forty looms were erected, after which, at different times, there were considerable additions made. In the year

1750, the number of looms stood at 100. Two hundred and fifty persons were employed in hacking, bleaching, warping, weaving, etc., and more than 500 spinners. There were houses and gardens for the master workmen, for which they did not pay any rent. The industry was said to be the largest in Ireland, with 172,116 yards of sailcloth manufactured over 1716 and 1717. A great part of this was exported to England, where the products of Douglas were held in great esteem. Samuel Perry was one of the village's leading lights, holding the position of chief director.

Belvelly Bricks

Belvelly Brickworks were in sporadic production from the 1850s until the First World War. Their origins may be linked to public health legislation hindering the burning of clay in the Brickfields (i.e. Lower Glanmire Road) and Douglas areas of Cork.

The Belvelly enterprise, situated near Potteries Cross, became at times so important that a special pier was erected west of Belvelly bridge, and a railway siding constructed south of Fota station. Belvelly bricks were transported to many parts of the world. Mallow-born writer, Irish patriot and businessman Denny Lane founded the Belvelly Brick Works. He was proprietor of Glyntown Distillery and established starch works in an inoperative five-storey woollen mill in Glanmire. His keen interest in enterprise led him to induce the other distilleries in Cork to merge under the title of Cork Distilleries Company. He was appointed a member of Cork Harbour Board, and later chairman of the Cork School of Science.

ESB Marina

The second of the ESB-led projects in 1950s Cork was that of the steam-powered station on the Marina (the first being the Lee Hydroelectric Scheme). Irish industry showed an overwhelming preference for electric power because of its availability, economy and convenience. The demand showed an increase of 49 million units in 1953, an increase of 47 per cent in the number of units used by consumers connected under rural electrification and a figure which strongly demonstrated the necessity for such extra electrical power. Every day, more and more farmers were making use of electricity for such everyday tasks as milking, churning, root pulping, grinding and so on.

Up to the late 1940s, power came from Ardnacrusha, Pigeon House on the Liffey, and Alleywood or Portarlington. In the event of Ardnacrusha not operating for any reason, power had to be transmitted over a long distance, which, experience had shown, was an unsatisfactory arrangement. Because of the Second World War, the preliminary work could not be undertaken until 1950, and the near completion of such a big undertaking in such as short space of time represented a notable achievement in its day.

Construction of the Marina station began in 1951. Operating from 1954, it fed electric power into the national network for use in homes, factories, streets, highways and farms throughout the south of Ireland. The station was the seventh power station to go into operation since the end of the war. For the preliminary development of the station, two 30,000kw steam turbo generating sets were installed. These gave an annual estimated output of 240 million units per year. These turbines were the biggest in use in Ireland and were of the latest two-cylinder type and generated electricity at 105kv. Transformers stepped up this figure to 110kv for easier transmission with minimum losses. A series of step-down transformers assisted in the ultimate delivery to the consumer at 220 volts. Steam was delivered to the two steam turbines at 850°F.

The Marina station occupied (and still does) a commanding location on a 13-acre site facing Cork quays. Surrounding it at one time was Messrs Henry Ford and Son's Motor assembly works, Dunlops Ltd rubber factory, the towering silos of the Cork Milling Co Ltd and National Flour Mills Ltd.

Whitegate Oil Refinery

Following on from the use of oil in the 1950s in the ESB Marina Power station, the petroleum industry in Ireland at that time was such a prodigious business that it was the costliest import and the greatest source of customs duty except tobacco. In January 1957, some 262 million gallons were imported at a cost of £13,667,000 (against approx £10½ million each for coal, motorcars, wheat and maize). As an offset, the government accepted the joint proposal of Shell-Mex and BP Ltd, Caltex and Esso to erect and to operate a new £12million refinery at Corkbeg Island, Whitegate, which was officially opened on 22 September 1959. Its annual capacity was initially proposed to supply Ireland's total petroleum needs.

The situation in Ireland was hardly dissimilar from the rest of Western Europe. Arising out of thinning coal seams and a manpower shortage, that had persisted since the end of the Second World War, industry was forced to turn to oil to bridge the gap between the growing demand and the capacity of native resources to provide it. Ireland's demand for electricity grew faster than the country's water power and turf resources could produce it. Industrial production was expanding. The era of cheap and plentiful supplies was over; they were insufficient to meet all demand. Oil was the only alternative.

On 29 November 1957, 2,200 people worked on the building of the new oil refinery at Whitegate. In addition, the refinery company had already recruited a staff of 120 for the permanent running of the facility, many of whom were being trained abroad but forty-three of whom were graduates of the National University. A large number of the fifty storage tanks being built by Tank Erectors Ltd were now complete, each with a capacity of 23,000 tons. Work was going ahead on the jetty head and the dolphins for the berthing of the tankers. Piping had been laid along the jetty for incoming and outgoing oil.

Since it opened in 1959, Ireland's only crude oil refinery has played a critical role in the country's energy infrastructure, supplying about 40 per cent of Ireland's transport and heating fuel. Whitegate is the country's only refinery. Today, the now-called Irving Whitegate Refinery processes light, low-sulphur crude oil, sourced from the North Sea and West Africa. The facility produces transportation and heating fuels such as gasoline, diesel and kerosene that are then distributed across Ireland and Europe.

Verolme Dockyard

In 1957, negotiations began with a Dutch firm for the establishment in Cork Harbour of a large-scale shipbuilding operation. The negotiations entered their final stages in October 1958 when Minister for Industry and Commerce Seán Lemass left for Holland on the invitation of Mr Cornelis Verolme, owner of Verolme United (an important ship building concern at Rotterdam, the largest port on the European continent).

Verolme United Shipyards was a concern with a worldwide reputation. It had large shipyards in the Netherlands at Alblasterdam, Meusden and Rosenburg, which could build and repair vessels up to 50,000 tons. An idea of the extent of Verolme United Shipyards' activities was given in a Dutch publication in 1958, which gave a listing of ships under construction or on order in shipyards in the Netherlands. It showed that Cornelis Verolme's three shipyards had more than any other single concern in Holland. It had on its order books thirty-six vessels, and of them twenty-five were tankers. One of them, being built for the Dutch Esso Company, was of 46,000 tons; three more, for American owners, were of 47,000 tons; two were 45,000 tons and six were 19,500 tons. Prior to opening in Rushbrooke, Verolme had successfully worked with the Brazilian government enabling him to build a shipyard in the Jacarecanga Bay near Rio de Janeiro.

Verolme occupied the site of the old yard at Rushbrooke, where ship repair work had been carried on for a century. The new yard covered a much larger area, a great deal of which was reclaimed from the estuary of the River Lee. The outstanding features of the new yard in 1960 were the huge 230ft-long plating shop and the new 668ft building slipway. The slipway was flanked by two giant mobile 40-ton cranes, which were used to transport the plates from the workshop to the slipway.

Under Verolme's stewardship, thirty-three ships were built in the dockyard, and at its peak, over 1,200 were employed. The shipbuilding industry in Ireland collapsed in the early 1980s and the dockyard closed in 1984. In 1995, the dockyard was purchased by the Doyle Group and renamed Cork Dockyard. The dockyard is now part of the Burke Shipping Group, the chief operating subsidiary of the Doyle Group. Burke Shipping is Ireland's leading shipping company, with facilities in all the major Irish ports. Some ship repair and marine and general engineering services are still carried out on the site, now named Cork Dockyard.

Irish Steel at Haulbowline

Haulbowline Steel Holdings was also a major player in Ireland's necklace of native industries. The site on Haulbowline Island was once the British naval dockyard where its docks were used for the loading and discharge of ships. In the Irish Free State the site belonged to the Board of Public Works but was developed by Hammond Lane Foundry in 1937.

In September 1937, 2,500 tons of plant and dismantled buildings, part of a steel mill at Charleroi, Belgium, were landed on Haulbowline Island for the works started there by the Hammond Lane Foundry Co Ltd, Dublin. The company had bought the whole mill. The new Haulbowline mill was to supply the Irish Free State's needs and was to export steel as well. Scrap being exported was to be diverted to the island for processing and pig-iron and coal were to be imported to the site. At the start, they planned to employ 1,000 in all. In June 1938, a new company, Irish Steel Ltd, was formed. There was also the deep-water basin and dock accommodation, which enabled the maximum advantage to be taken of the cheapest method to get raw material to, and finished product from, the mills.

Fast forward to 8 January 1947, and Irish Steel Ltd was placed in the hands of a receiver. Shortly afterwards, the Irish government took it over as a going concern. Between 1947 and 1957, the annual production of ingots and bars quadrupled, the increase being particularly marked during 1956 and 1957. Steel was sold competitively in New Zealand, India, South Africa, Finland, Greece, Jamaica, Trinidad, Guinea, the Philippines, Cyprus, Iraq, Sudan, Kuwait and Malaya.

During the post-war years of the 1950s, a distinctive feature of the steel industry throughout the world was the rapid expansion of production capacity. By September 1958, an extensive programme of expansion of the operations of Irish Steel Holdings was proposed, incorporating an additional 200 workers on top of 450 workers. The development proposals comprised the expansion of its open-hearth furnace capacity, the casting of large ingots, which were to be rolled in a new building into a wide range of finished and semi-finished sections, and the adaptation and mechanisation of existing steel-making processes.

Haulbowline Island was connected to the mainland in 1968. ISPAT leased the operation from the government in 1996 and increased production. By 2001, when the operation went into liquidation, the steel production plant and allied activities, including a galvanized steel production unit, occupied 11.ha. The main fabrication building was demolished in 2006 as part of a clean-up of the site ordered by the Department of the Environment. An Irish government decision was made to provide a total of €61 million to remediate the location from a former waste site at the eastern tip, to become a large public amenity park to open in 2019.

Ringaskiddy Industrial Development

In the late 1960s, the Ringaskiddy area was chosen as the area most suitable for intensive industrial development in accordance with the £10 million development plan by Cork Harbour Commissioners. The report detailed that the area of Ringaskiddy being developed to accommodate a wide range of industries was at a relatively lower cost than the Whitegate area.

On 13 September 1968, the multi-million dollar Pfizer Group of New York announced an £8 million investment into setting up a chemical plant at Ringaskiddy. Pfizer is a worldwide organisation, engaged in the manufacture of products for medicines and industry. It had eighty-four factories in thirty-two countries and employs hundreds of thousands of workers throughout the world.

The Cork project was to include the construction of a jetty capable of handling ocean-going ships of up to 20,000 tons. Citric acid was used increasingly in food and soft drink production and in the manufacture of pharmaceuticals. Industrial uses for citric and gluconic acid and their derivatives were expanding, notably for cleaning purposes. The Irish raw materials included lime, sulphuric acid and beet molasses. Pfizer's decision to locate their plant in Ireland was made because the grants and other incentives made available by the Republic offered the most favourable return on invested capital.

Cork estuary was geographically well situated in relation to supplies of raw materials and shipment of finished goods to world markets. Adequate power and water supplies were available and an educated and adaptable labour force was also available. The site also allowed ample room for expansion.

For many years, Ringaskiddy lay at the end of a road on the edge of Cork Harbour. By 1970, the same physical road led on to Haulbowline Island with its busy steel rolling mills and naval depot, and a new road, rerouted from Shanbally, began to serve the rising Pfizer Chemical Corporation plant, a source of much employment for construction workers that soon was to begin its own intake of skilled technicians.

When the Pfizer plant officially opened in October 1972 it produced a range of products derived from citric and gluconic acid. Its plant at Ringaskiddy would eventually occupy 170 acres, making the Cork project the group's biggest organic chemical manufacturing facility outside the USA.

By 1986, Ringaskiddy was the centre of pharmachemical production in Cork, and perhaps Ireland. Novartis developed a 40-hectare site in the early 1990s, and existing facilities were upgraded, such as those of Pfizer and ADM.

Ringaskiddy is an important industrial centre, particularly for pharmaceutical companies such as Centocor, GlaxoSmithKline, Hovione, Novartis, Pfizer and Recordati. Ringaskiddy port handles much of the vehicle imports for the southern part of Ireland.

National Maritime College

For several centuries nautical training was informally taught in Ireland in various forms – the most common being an apprenticeship. In Dublin in 1889, nautical education was offered in a formal way with the end result being the receiving by participants of Certificates of Competency. Fast forward to 1975, and the Department of Education opted that all maritime training would be pursued at the Cork Regional Technical College (RTC). The Irish Nautical College, and some of its staff and equipment, transferred to Cork.

By the late 1990s, there was strong competition for space in the Bishopstown campus coupled with the need to adopt the STCW95 Code of the International Maritime Organisation. The code laid out the minimum standards for training seafarers especially in areas of lifesaving and survival training and simulation facilities.

The Department of Nautical Studies at Cork Institute of Technology (previously Cork Regional Technical College) sought to comply with the code.

Likewise, in the Naval Service, training accommodation and facilities were in need of upgrading. The management of the navy also sought that naval officers should become compliant with the provisions of the STCW95 code.

Informal discussion began between naval officers and CIT staff, which led to a draft joint scheme of resolution. More formal discussions quickly ensued, and a meeting was arranged between Mr Donal Burke, Head of Nautical Studies at CIT, and Commodore John Kavanagh, Flag Officer Commanding the Naval Service. Soon after a formal proposal was given to government, which has also asked that the Department of Defence site at Ringaskiddy be developed as a joint college as the National Maritime College of Ireland. It opened in 2004.

Marina Point

Marino Point, Cobh, was originally owned by Colonel Stuart French, who lived in an adjoining estate. It initially opened as Nitrigin Eireann Teoranta in 1979 and manufactured ammonia and urea. It was taken over eight years later by Irish Fertiliser Industries (IFI) in a joint venture with the British-based Imperial Chemical Industries. It closed in 2002 with the loss of 220 jobs. In early August 2017, the Port of Cork secured the former Irish Fertiliser Industries Plant at Cobh in a public-private partnership deal that will see a significant expansion of its cargo handling facilities. The approximately €6 million deal with Wexford-based Lanber Holdings gives the port a 40 per cent stake in the site of the Marino Point plant.

Lee Tunnel

Ireland's largest road project promised to revolutionise economic and social life in Cork and brought with it considerable expectation and a long list of ambitious and expensive goals. Earmarked at its opening on 21 May 1999 as the most significant piece of a £105 million jigsaw, the Lee Tunnel, it was hoped, would free up movement in and out of the city centre, reduce overall congestion levels and allow traffic to bypass key routes. Linking the Dunkettle road network on the north side of the city with Ringmahon point on the south side, the 620m tunnel was designed to divert a significant volume of traffic, particularly heavy vehicles, away from the city centre routes. River dredging work began in 1996 to prepare the trench for the six-unit tunnel beneath the river bed, which was 20m below the tide level at its deepest point. The six units were manoeuvred into place inside a casting basin using temporary water ballasts, and sunk into position under the river bed. The timing of the immense operation was very much dictated by the tide, giving planners less than 48 hours in which to tow, sink and secure each unit into place. The whole operation was completed over a five-week period.

   Over 500,000 cubic metres of silt, alluvium and gravel, and 80,000 cubic metres of limestone rock on the southern shoreline was used in the construction of the five tunnel tubes and the approach road. The tunnel has a structural life of 120 years.

The Challenges of the Blue Economy

On 11 July 2016, a state-of-the-art maritime facility, UCC's Beaufort building in Ringaskiddy, opened. Created to focus on the energy power and business of the Blue Economy (marine-related economic prospects with a preservational slant), the press releases of the day to the media described an impressive space – a '4,700m-squared five-storey Beaufort building with state-of-the-art wave simulators, test tanks, workshops and offices provides Ireland with world-class infrastructure for renewable energy and maritime research'. The building was named after the Irish hydrographer Rear Admiral Sir Francis Beaufort, who influenced the creation of a globally adopted Beaufort wind force scale.

At the time of writing the Beaufort building houses the SFI MaREI Centre (Marine Renewable Energy Ireland) and the LIR National Ocean Test Facility. The SFI MaREI centre caters for 135 researchers, industry partners and support staff, dedicated to solving the challenges related to marine renewable energy. From 2010 to 2017, the building also housed Ireland's Maritime Energy Research Cluster, which inspired further research platforms into the Blue Economy.

10

RECREATION
AND TOURISM

Royal Cork Yacht Club

The Royal Cork Yacht Club (RCYC) traces its origins back to 1720. It began with the establishment, by six worthies of the time, of the Water Club of the Harbour of Cork, headquartered in the castle of Haulbowline Island. Membership was limited to twenty-five, and strict protocol governed all the club's activities, both afloat and ashore. One rule, for example, ordered 'that no boat presume to sail ahead of the Admiral, or depart the fleet without his orders, but may carry what sail he please to keep company'. Another forbade the Admiral to bring more than 'two dozen (bottles of) wine to his treat'. The rules were applied with some rigour by the founding six members, who formed the club's committee in 1720.

The six are believed to have been 24-year-old William, the 4th Earl of Inchiquin, and probably the first Admiral of the club; the Honourable James O'Brien, brother of the Admiral; Charles O'Neill of Shanes Court, County Antrim, who settled in Midleton and married Catherine, a daughter of the Rt Hon St Broderick of Midleton; Rev Richard Bullen, who later became the club chaplain; and Henry Mitchell and John Rogers, about whom nothing is known. Racing proper did not begin until 1787 and, in the years prior to that, the club's members contented themselves with sailing in a rather leisurely fashion around the harbour once a month from April to September on the spring tide.

The club enjoyed great popularity right through the nineteenth century and well into the twentieth, and promoted the annual Cork Harbour Regatta. However, by the 1950s, with its Cobh clubhouse in a poor location on the harbour and with no sheltered or secure moorings, the end seemed in sight for this historic club. In 1957, however, the Royal Munster Yacht Club and the Royal Cork agreed to merge and took up the invitation of the Cork Harbour Motor Boat Club to move to its premises in Crosshaven. The new club gained the most enthusiastic and interested members of all three founding clubs and was thus placed on a genuinely firm footing.

Today, the RCYC is established as one of the world's leading yacht clubs and its biennial regatta – now known as Cork Week – is regarded as one of the premier such events in the world. The club is acknowledged for its excellence in race management on the water and this, combined with a very professional shore-side approach, has resulted in attracting many major sailing events to Crosshaven.

Bowling at Castlemary

The sport of road bowling has a long connection with County Cork. A painting by Daniel McDonald from 1842 is entitled *Bowling Match at Castlemary, Cloyne*. It is the possession of the Crawford Municipal Art Gallery, Cork. It shows a mid-nineteenth century bowling match. The bowlers depicted are reputed to be Abraham Morris, a leading Cork businessman and Orangeman, and Montiford Longfield, likewise an Orangeman. This narrative is unusual as the participation of such establishment figures in bowling in the nineteenth century is a strange one. Local police viewed the game as dangerous on public roads and Bowl players regularly found themselves in trouble with the law.

Royal Victoria Baths, Glenbrook

The Royal Victoria Baths were opened in 1838. The baths were tremendously popular with the people of Cork. The hot salt water was believed to be invigorating and a valuable treatment for rheumatism, lumbago and similar complaints. During the nineteenth century, the baths were probably Cork's most popular seaside resort. Towards the end of the century, other destinations further down the harbour became increasingly accessible by river steamer and the baths began to lose their popularity. They closed around the turn of the century and were derelict by 1929.

Queenstown, the Health Resort

In the nineteenth century, Queenstown was promoted as a health resort on account of its climate and location and was on par with Bournemouth in the south of England and Ventnor on the Isle of Wight. The promenade on the water's edge is a favourite place for locals and visitors to relax. The bandstand was originally built for the visit of Queen Victoria in August 1849. During the summer months regular band recitals take place there. The two cannon on the promenade were returned from the Boer and Crimean Wars in 1899 and 1854, respectively. Later, the promenade was named after US President John F. Kennedy.

The Victorious Goalers

The Victorious Goalers of Carrigaline and Kilmoney is a rare Cork Harbour ballad, which tells of hurling games played long before the GAA came into being. On 17 December 1828, a local team from Carrigaline and Kilmoney defeated a team from the neighbouring parish of Shanbally-Ringaskiddy. Such matches were not infrequently organised by local landlords and in this case the team from Shanbally was led by William Connor, a naval officer of Ballybricken House (now demolished). The venue was Cope's Field, a large field north-east of Carrigaline Castle. The 'goal', as the contest was termed (in Irish, *baire*), was conducted according to rules similar to the present GAA ones. There were eighteen to twenty players a side, the *sliotar* covered with stitched leather, an agreed referee, marked endlines and a change of sides at halftime.

Rowing in the Harbour

Cork Harbour Rowing Club was founded in the Victoria Hotel, Glenbrook, on April 1859, and in the following year the first regatta took place with crews from London and Glasgow taking part. Large sums of money were wagered on the races, which included four-oared gigs, and one of the courses was 3 miles from Ringaskiddy up to Passage and back to Glenbrook. One of the club's earliest vessels was *The Dream*. In 1865, Cork Harbour Rowing Club bought its first racing eight, *Laura*, which is accepted as being the first of its kind in Ireland, and in the same year the club had the honour of being the first in the country to row an outrigged boat called *The Vision*. Two years later, the crew of a Cork Harbour Rowing Club four won two races at the prestigious London Regatta, and in 1872 at Glenbrook Regatta Shannon Rowing Club won the Glenbrook Cup for the first time in Ireland with a boat with sliding seats. The early enthusiasm was not maintained and the club gradually became a social more than a rowing club. The situation was not helped by a split in 1868, which resulted in many rowers joining the Queen's College Rowing Club, formed in Cork the same year.

Rowing ceased in 1929 and the club itself ceased to function by 1936 but bridging a gap of almost forty years at the revival ceremony in 1968 were surviving members of the last crews to row: Fergus Cross, Joe Kavanagh, Frank Byrne, Tom O'Gorman, Bob Patterson, Billy Collins and Dermot Dixon.

Today some of the harbour's other historic clubs operate strongly – from the city to the harbour mouth – Christian Brothers College Rowing Club, Shandon Boat Club, Lee Rowing Club, Cork Boat Club, Naomh Ógra Chorcaí, Blackrock Rowing Club, Passage West Rowing Club, East Ferry Rowing Club, and Whitegate Rowing Club.

The Woods of Currabinny

It is strange but true that in the eighteenth century Currabinny was completely devoid of trees. It was let out in small farms divided into tiny fields and presumably was cultivated right to the top of the hill. Arthur Young, the English agriculturalist, visited Coolmore in 1776 and wrote as follows: 'Rode to the mouth of Cork Harbour; the grounds about it are all fine, bold and varied, but so bare of trees that there is not a single view but that pains one for want of wood.' In the early nineteenth century an enlightened landowner decided to plant the whole headland. Antiquarian and writer John Windele, in 1849, recorded that the headland had been recently planted. By the end of the century, it is described as being thickly covered with trees. By then, too, it had become a select residential resort and several new villas as well as a massive terrace fronted the shore.

In the 1880s, Currabinny belonged to James Lane of Myrtleville Cottage (now Bunnyconnellan Restaurant), a member of the Cork brewing family. His grandson, Sir Hugh Lane, became renowned as an art collector, and was a victim of the *Lusitania* sinking in 1915. By July 1969, the 90 acres of scenic woodland were sold by the Hobart Estate to the Irish Forestry Division. The woods are stocked with broadleaved trees, mainly beech, oak, sycamore, ash and birch. It also has some Scots pine and Corsican pine, which were planted *c*.1965. Other flora includes a selection of flowering shrubs and ornamental trees. Another interesting feature of the woods is the elegant octagonal gazebo tea house in the centre, which a previous private landowner had built for tea with a view.

Lower Aghada Tennis and Sailing Club

Established in 1917, the Lower Aghada Tennis and Sailing Club originally played in the Careystown area of Whitegate. In 1921 the club bought the 3 1/2 acre site of the old First World War American Air Base at a small sum of £5 from the Land Commission. Ten people from the area each contributed 10/- (50p) each, and two trustees, Messrs Terence Murphy, NT and Edmund Russell.

The actual playing surface was on the remains of the old runways. In 1960 the club came in for another lucky streak of fortune when Cork County Council was building the new Midleton – Whitegate road. The proposed new road was to go through the old tennis courts and the county council transferred the courts to the present site, where it also built a new clubhouse.

In the 1970s there were numerous developments and members started to make a strong impact in competitions. It was decided in view of the fact that membership was increasing at such a rapid pace to further develop the site and so a decision was taken to provide an additional three courts. In 1980 another court was added.

Throughout the 1980s the club was the 'flagship' of Irish tennis. It was the first rural club in Ireland to install tournament-standard floodlighting. It ran some of the more prestigious tournaments and its players competed at the highest level. The culmination of this work was the construction of an ultra-modern clubhouse in the late 1980s.

The most recent development was formally opened on 29 March 2015 by Minister Michael Ring TD. This mammoth project involved resurfacing all six courts, reconstruction of courts five and six, reconstruction of half court four, putting all electrical services underground, a complete redesign and the installation of new floodlights. Due to a fire destroying the clubhouse on 13 June 2017 temporary accommodation in the form of a portacabin was utilised.

Ford Boxes and Holiday Home

In the late 1800s, Crosshaven flourished from a quiet backwater into a tourism resort. The numerous bays such as Graball Bay were unrivalled for bathing accommodation – even bathing dresses and towels could be obtained. One media story records a local lady who erected two comfortable tents which could dine at least fifty people and which were in constant demand. By the 1930s, the area had witnessed many light wooden holiday bungalows constructed by Cork's citizens. Many were constructed from disused Ford delivery crates for cars in the mid-twentieth century.

Ford Boxes were salvaged from the Ford factory on the Marina and sold en mass after they had been used to ship motor parts over from Dagenham. Hard and enduring, the boxes became a marvel around Cork and were used as dog kennels, fowl houses, pigeon lofts, piggeries, flooring for trailers, boxes for storing grain, and even dancing platforms.

Crosshaven AFC

Founded by the British Army Garrison that was based in Fort Camden, the club held its first AGM on Tuesday 13 September 1898 in Camden – thereby making it one of the oldest surviving soccer clubs in Munster.

Crosshaven AFC began as a minor team and shortly after this fielded a juvenile eleven. The first pitch was at Noonan's Boreen between the roads to Graball Bay and Church Bay. Four subsequent pitches were within a short distance of each other near St Patrick's Cemetery, and for a time matches were played on or near the present grounds. Crosshaven's pitch for many years, affectionately known as the The Bog, was acquired primarily for juveniles in 1959. Crosshaven AFC finally returned to Camden in the 1980s, where the club has remained ever since.

In the 1930s the club went up a grade to junior. Due to a shortage of players during 'The Emergency', senior and junior ranks in Cork were combined and during this period Crosshaven won the Munster Shield (1941–42).

Crosshaven were also the first winners of the Ancient Order of Hibernian Cup in the season 1951–52 and reached the Cork Area final of the FAI Junior Cup, losing after three matches to Maymount. They went unbeaten for eighteen months. In the mid-1950s, Crosshaven entered the Munster Senior League and quickly made an impact by winning the Beamish Cup and Burkley Cup in 1955.

Some of the senior players went on to League of Ireland clubs and others retired, so the decision was made to return to junior ranks. Nevertheless, soccer was thriving and in 1960 a schoolboys' section was set up. Both the juniors and youths enjoyed success during that decade, reaching nine finals and winning seven.

In 1972, the following year, the club decided to re-enter the Munster Senior League and so began another glorious chapter in the club's history. Within a few years, Crosshaven won every honour at that grade, including the Munster Senior League, the Elvery Cup, the Lawson Cup, the Pop Kelleher Cup, and they reached the final of the 1980 Munster Senior FA Cup, losing to League of Ireland side Cork United. They were also the first club to win the Keane Cup in 1979 and retained it the next year.

For a couple of years in the 1980s, Crosshaven also fielded a ladies' team, which came second in Division II of the Cork League and reached the final of the League Cup. The boys under-age section was revived in 1983. Over the past seven decades, many Crosshaven players have gone on to play soccer in the League of Ireland.

The Majorca Ballroom

The big news of Thursday 30 May 1963 was the opening of a lavish new ballroom in Crosshaven. It was built on the most modern lines and was the brainchild of brothers Jer and Murt Lucey, who also owned the Redbarn Ballroom in Youghal, with a number of chalets and a fully equipped caravan park.

There was to be dancing space for over 2,000 and the soft, subdued lighting and lush decor took quite a lot of thought and planning. One of the features of the ballroom was its revolving stage. The first to take the stage were Clipper Carlton and Michael O'Callaghan. The Majorca was followed in 1968 by the creation by the Lucey Brothers of the Stardust Club Hotel on the Grand Parade, Cork City.

The building and site of the Majorca ballroom was bought in July 1995. The building was dismantled and the site taken into enlarging the adjacent boatyard.

Sirius Arts Centre

Sirius Arts Centre is a multidisciplinary non-profit centre for the arts in the East Cork area. Founded in 1988, the former Royal Cork Yacht Club premises in Cobh was transformed into an arts centre. The magnificent nineteenth-century building on the seafront was purchased from University College Cork by Sirius Commemoration Ltd, a non-profit company formed to mark the first transatlantic steamship crossing. The committee launched a high-powered fundraising campaign aimed at raising the cost of purchasing and renovating the hallowed old clubhouse.

A Fishing Hub

Since 2009, Fáilte Ireland and the Central Fisheries Board have selected Cork Harbour as a Centre of Angling Excellence. Tourist literature celebrate what is described as 'reef, wreck and shore fishing' and how regular anglers regularly find 'specimen-sized fish, including bass, red gurnard, golden grey mullet, thick-lipped mullet, whiting and blue shark'.

Cork Harbour Festival

Initiated in 1993, Meitheal Mara (Community or Workers from the Sea) is a community boatyard located at Crosses Green on the south bank of the River Lee. With energetic and enthusiastic staff,

Naval Boat Race, 1865, from *Illustrated London News* (source: Cork City Library)

the group grew in status. In 2005, they launched the Ocean to City rowing race from the outer harbour to the city's quays. The concept was and still is to bring together traditional fixed seats comprising everything from boats, currachs to skiffs. Every year the event goes from strength to strength.

In 2008, Cork Harbour Day was created by committee members representing UCC, City and County Councils and the Port of Cork.

By 2015, An Rás Mór and Cork Harbour Open Day existed as two popular one-day events situated at different points in Cork's annual maritime calendar. Both event committees recognised the need to work together and began to work together and share resources.

As a result, in 2015, Cork Harbour Festival was launched. The festival was framed on the principle that An Rás Mór would be the flagship event and a whole series of mini events would be built around it in the days before and after it.

Annually, there are nine festival days starting in the first week of June. In general, there are over forty different event partners in Cork City as well as in the towns and villages along Cork Harbour. The programme aims to highlight Cork's rich heritage and culture as well as water and shore-based activities. The Cork Harbour Festival Committee comprises representatives from Cork City Council, Cork County Council, Port of Cork, UCC, MaREI, RCYC, Cobh Harbour Chamber, IMERC and Meitheal Mara.